T0356010

BEST OF MEXICAN COOKING

BEST OF
MEXICAN
COOKING

75 AUTHENTIC HOME-STYLE RECIPES
FOR BEGINNERS

ADRIANA MARTIN

PHOTOGRAPHY BY HÉLÈNE DUJARDIN

ROCKRIDGE
PRESS

For general information on our other products and services or to obtain technical support, please contact our Customer Care Department within the United States at (866) 744-2665, or outside the United States at (510) 253-0500.

Rockridge Press publishes its books in a variety of electronic and print formats. Some content that appears in print may not be available in electronic books, and vice versa.

TRADEMARKS: Rockridge Press and the Rockridge Press logo are trademarks or registered trademarks of Callisto Media Inc. and/or its affiliates, in the United States and other countries, and may not be used without written permission. All other trademarks are the property of their respective owners. Rockridge Press is not associated with any product or vendor mentioned in this book.

Interior and Cover Designer: Eric Pratt
Art Producer: Hannah Dickerson
Editor: Gurvinder Singh Gandu
Production Editor: Matthew Burnett
Production Manager: Holly Haydash

Photography © 2021 Hélène Dujardin; food styling by Anna Hampton.
Author photograph courtesy of Geisha Barazarte, Creativa Photography.

Cover: Pozole, page 62

Hardcover ISBN: 978-1-63878-631-3
Paperback ISBN: 978-1-64876-569-8
eBook ISBN: 978-1-64876-570-4
R0

I DEDICATE THIS BOOK TO MY ABUELA ALICIA AND MY MOM, ROSA ELENA. THEY TAUGHT ME THAT LOVE IS THE MAIN INGREDIENT OF AN EXCELLENT HOME-COOKED MEAL.

CONTENTS

INTRODUCTION

I was born in the state of Tamaulipas but raised in Mexico City. My mom, Rosa Elena, was from Chihuahua, and my father, José, was from Tabasco but with Lebanese roots. My great-grandmother, Doña Carlota (lovingly called Mamá Grande), was from Sonora, and my great-grandfather, Don Rafael, was a businessman from Chihuahua. My grandmother Alicia (Mamá Licha), a former opera singer, married Papá Angel, a Spanish refugee who became my grandfather. So, I grew up experiencing a variety of cultures and dishes from regions throughout Mexico, from the North to the South, and all the way to the Middle East and Spain.

I remember days in La Colonia del Valle in Mexico City, playing with dough while Mamá Grande made fresh flour tortillas to pair with her popular pozole Sonorense. I can still smell the spices and feel the warmth of her kitchen.

Mamá Licha was a restauranteur and my great-grandfather owned a beer company and a hotel, so I was exposed to the hospitality industry and a commercial kitchen at an early age. I grew up near a stove, and my hobby was reading cookbooks and culinary dictionaries.

Mamá Licha loved my company and I cherished every moment I spent with her in that huge kitchen, where she'd set up a small table with a chair and kid-friendly utensils to teach me how to peel a potato. Shopping with her at El Mercado de La Merced and Mercado de San Juan taught me the importance of choosing the best ingredients for making the best dishes.

Aunt Julieta was my grandmother's sister, and her specialty was baking and stews. She made the best tortitas de papa, beef caldillo, and sopapillas. My mouth is watering just thinking about them!

Living in Mexico City, I experienced local dishes that my family typically didn't prepare at home but that I would eat at friends' houses. Tamales, chilaquiles, huaraches, tlacoyos, and nopalitos were some of my favorites.

My dream was to become a chef, but I ended up embracing a marketing profession instead. Through the years, my passion for cooking grew and a need for a creative platform became a priority. I decided to take professional cooking, food styling, and photography classes and became a food writer and professional recipe developer in the United States, where I currently live. Since then, I have published thousands of recipes, between collaborations with leading brands and my recipe site, AdrianasBestRecipes.com. As an immigrant, keeping my roots alive makes me feel connected to the place I came from, and food has been the best way for me to connect to my land and my most treasured family memories.

I am so excited to share my first cookbook with you. It includes many of my family's recipes and beloved homestyle recipes bursting with Mexico's authentic flavors. Mexico has a vast culinary history, and whether you are new to home cooking or already a lover of Mexican food, you will find classic recipes from Mexico's many culinary regions (no Tex-Mex here). Each recipe includes a brief history of the dish's origin and different interpretations depending on the region.

All recipes use modern cooking techniques and offer substitutes for classic ingredients that might not be readily available.

THE WORLD OF MEXICAN COOKING

In this chapter, you will learn a bit about Mexico's many culinary regions and some foundational ingredients of Mexican cooking, such as chiles, condiments, and herbs that are typically found in Mexican home kitchens. There's also a list of equipment needed for cooking authentic Mexican meals and a guide for roasting and toasting vegetables and peppers to develop the fabulous smoky flavors characteristic of many favorite Mexican dishes.

THE CULINARY REGIONS OF MEXICO

Mexican cooking is diverse and complex. The ancient Maya and Aztec civilizations' diets, from which it descends, included corn, game meats, fish, cacao, and chiles. During the Spanish conquest, other ingredients such as wheat, pork, dairy products, and spices were introduced. The combination of these cultures created what we know now as Mexican cuisine.

Spanish nuns also played their part. Nuns used traditional Spanish recipes from the Old World and incorporated local ingredients to substitute for those not found in the New World. That is how mestizo cooking was born. Examples of fusion or mestizo dishes include tinga and mole.

Mexican cuisine varies according to the region. For example, in the North, the foods produced are mainly beef, dairy, wheat, and corn. Thus, in Northern Mexican–inspired cuisine, these ingredients take center stage. In the South, however, typical dishes include fish, bananas, and other tropical ingredients that are abundant there. But no matter the region, what unites them all is the love that home cooks incorporate when preparing each dish.

THE NORTH

The North comprises Sonora, Coahuila, Chihuahua, Durango, Baja California, Tamaulipas, Nuevo Leon, Zacatecas, and Aguascalientes. This area is ranching country. Cattle, grains, and dairy are the primary sources of food; therefore, beef, milk, and cheese are the main proteins. Corn plays a critical role in the diet, including sweet drinks such as pinole and savory soups made of dried corn and chile colorado. Grilled steaks, alambres, and the popular dried meat called machaca are popular among working families. A variety of cheeses, including the famous Chihuahua asadero and queso ranchero, are widespread, too. Also unique from the North are the different types of flour tortillas made there (a whopping 40 types between savory and sweet!). For example, Sonora's flour tortillas are thin and large, whereas Chihuahua's are small and thick. Sonorans' favorite treats are coyotas, hand pies made of dough, milk, and sugar and filled with shredded piloncillo.

NORTH PACIFIC COAST

The states of the North Pacific Coast include Sinaloa, Colima, Jalisco, and Nayarit. This region is known for its agriculture, and it is where most of Mexico's staples such as tomatoes, grains, and chiles are produced. The region is also known for its abundance of seafood from the Pacific Ocean: sailfish, swordfish, amberjack tuna, and snapper, to mention just a few. The geographic location and the combination of land and sea influence the local cuisine. Sinaloa is the home of aguachile, the chilorio, and the marlin, while Jalisco is famous for its birria, tortas ahogadas, and tequila. In Nayarit, the frijoles puercos are a typical treat for parties and family gatherings; this dish's main ingredient is frijoles azufrados, a bean that is characteristic of the North Pacific Coast and one of its culinary staples.

SOUTH PACIFIC COAST

The South Pacific Coast of Mexico has miles and miles of sandy beaches, mountainous tropical forests, rugged lands, and rocky cliffs. Agriculture and tourism are the main economic activities in the region, which comprises the states of Oaxaca, Chiapas, and Guerrero. This area has remained populated by the Mixtec and Zapotec cultures, and the cuisine has embraced those indigenous roots by keeping traditional cooking techniques and ingredients. Oaxaca is the home of mole negro and chocolate, Chiapas is known for classic tamales and enfrijoladas, and Guerrero for pozole blanco and pescado a la talla.

BAJÍO

The Bajío region contains the Michoacán, Guanajuato, Queretaro, and San Luis Potosí states. The region is located in the northwest center of Mexico, near the Lerma River. This area is considered the breadbasket of Mexico, as it produces wheat, corn, beans, peanuts, and strawberries. This region was home to the first Spanish colony, and that legacy has influenced the customs and local cuisine. This includes the introduction of pork and dairy, which is why Michoacán is famous for its carnitas and cotija cheese. Guanajuato is known for its strawberries, cajeta, arroz con leche, buñuelos, and enchiladas mineras, San Luis Potosí for its queso de tuna, and Querétaro for its enchiladas.

CENTRAL MEXICO

Central Mexico, the Mexican Altiplano, is important for its vast geographical area and population. This region, which includes Puebla, Morelos, Tlaxcala, Hidalgo, and Mexico City, has the largest share of agricultural production, industry, and mineral wealth. Nuns who cooked for the Spanish viceroy created the current staples. Poblano mole and chiles en nogada were invented in Puebla, along with desserts and baked goods inspired by Spanish cuisine. Hidalgo is the home of mixiotes, a pre-hispanic cuisine favorite. While Morelos was the home for the chichimecas and tecpanecas civilizations. After the Spanish conquest, missionaries incorporated crops such as sugarcane, roses from Castile, and various tubers. Morelos now produces many of the ornamental plants found in gardens all over Mexico. Some classic dishes from Morelos include cecina de Yecapixtla, café de olla, agua ardiente liquor, and picadillo-stuffed peppers. In Mexico City, one of the most populous cities in the world, life is fast; street food is everywhere. Taquerías and barbacoa are part of the local culture. Many cultures converge there; however, there are staple dishes that everyone cooks at home: chicken soup, fideo seco, and enchiladas, plus the baked goods, tamales, and drinks typical for special occasions.

THE GULF

Tabasco and Veracruz belong to the Gulf of Mexico. Both states share the petroleum industry. Hernán Cortés founded Veracruz under the name "La Villa Rica de la Vera Cruz." This state has the most Caribbean and Creole influences, and its cuisine is a mix of Afro-Cuban and Spanish. The region's staple dish is pescado a la veracruzana, a Spanish-Creole fusion using red snapper, olives, European spices, tomato sauce, and chiles. Peanuts are commonly used in dishes such as encacahuatado de pollo, a peanut sauce with chiles. Plantains, yucca, and sweet potatoes are often served as side dishes. Café con leche, picaditas, and gorditas infladas with black beans are breakfast favorites. Tabasco is famous for its lush rainforests, wetlands, rivers, and lakes; this state is home to cacao, which once was used as currency. The Olmec culture was prevalent in the Gulf region; in fact, Olmecs developed the chocolate confection, but the Mayas perfected it by mixing cocoa beans with spices, chiles, and water. Tabasco has an abundance of crayfish and crab, not to mention other fish species such as the pejelagarto (tropical gar, known as Tabasco's swamp fish). Families cook this fish in soups, tamales, and grilled.

The South is where the Yucatán Peninsula, Campeche, and Quintana Roo are located. The region is recognized for its biological diversity and cultural wealth. Yucatán is known mostly for its tropical rainforest, jungles, cenotes, beaches, and the Maya culture. The primary industry is tourism; however, agriculture and citrus crops are also important. Yucatán's culinary culture is distinct from the rest of Mexico, as it is a mixture of Maya, Cuban, Caribbean, Middle Eastern, and European influences. Annatto, produced in this region, is the main spice in pibil dishes. Various recado seasonings and habaneros are used for making classic dishes, such as chirmole, relleno negro, and pavo en escabeche. In Campeche, yellowtail amberjack, smalltooth sawfish, and cazón are some of the fish used in dishes such as pan de cazón, a layered grilled fish dish. Quintana Roo is a well-known tourist spot with Cancún, but it also produces the Maya liqueur, Xtabentún, made with fermented honey and anise. The cuisine of the South is heavily inspired by the Maya culture, and salbutes, panuchos, and papatzules are part of the regular home menu.

INDIGENOUS COOKING TRADITIONS

Mexican cuisine is a vibrant part of the country's cultural heritage. Authentic Mexican food derives from the combination of ancient Mesoamerican and Spanish cuisines. (The Mesoamerican cultures include Zapotec, Mixtec, Mexica or Aztec, and Nahua.)

The Zapotecs and Mixtecs are based in Oaxaca. Many of them still speak the ancient languages and not Spanish. We have the Zapotecs to thank for introducing the comal for cooking tortillas and memelas, but they also contributed a diversity of mole sauces, which is the reason Oaxaca is called "the land of the seven moles." Some moles are influenced by Mixtec culture (e.g., mole negro and mole blanco) and others by Zapotec (e.g., ceremonial mole zapoteco). Abigail Mendoza is one of the most famous Zapotec chefs. You might recall her from an episode of *Parts Unknown*, where she made a special meal for Anthony Bourdain.

continued >

The Aztecs were of Nahua ethnicity, but the Nahua people were dedicated to agriculture while the Aztecs were warriors. The Nahua and Aztec culinary legacy includes several uses of corn and the nix-tamalization technique, a traditional process for treating, drying, and grinding corn to make masa harina for tortillas.

In the South, the Mayas invented the pib, an outdoor oven made with dirt and hot stones or clay balls. They would wrap marinated meat in banana leaves and cook it underground for several hours. They also used natural substances to create seasonings for marinades, such as annatto paste and various recados, to use in different meals, such as relleno negro and chirmole.

THE MEXICAN PANTRY

The ingredients that form the Mexican pantry are diverse. A well-stocked Mexican pantry includes staples such as herbs, spices, garlic, dried chiles, grains, legumes, classic seasonings, maize (corn), and fresh produce. Although you will be able to find many of these ingredients at a standard grocery store, some ingredients may require a trip to a specialty market.

FRESH FRUITS, VEGETABLES, AND HERBS

Good Mexican home cooking uses local ingredients that are simple and fresh, making good use of what's in season. Many of the ingredients listed here form the foundation of Mexican homecooked meals.

Avocados

The most common type of Mexican avocado is called aguacate Hass (Hass avocado). This crop comes from Michoacán, a state with volcanic soil and the perfect weather to grow avocados. However, Oaxaca, Guanajuato, Jalisco,

Guerrero, Chiapas, and Veracruz also grow the crop. Mexican avocados are creamy and suitable for guacamole and other sauces. Firmer avocados serve as garnishes for salads and ceviches, and they can be stuffed with salad variations. The ripeness can be determined by the color and how firm it feels to the touch. You can also check by removing the stem; if the inside looks green, it is ready to eat. If it looks dark, it is past its prime.

Avocado Leaf
This common ingredient is used for adding flavor and aroma to beans. It can also be used to wrap chunks of meat and tamales, and it can be a replacement for corn tortillas when grilled.

Cilantro
Also known as coriander, cilantro is an indispensable ingredient for pico de gallo and is used in raw sauces, soups, and as a garnish for tacos and carnitas, among other things. Authentic Mexican food requires cilantro's characteristic flavor.

Epazote
The epazote is an aromatic plant used since pre-Hispanic times. Black beans and esquites take on a unique flavor when accompanied by this herb. Fresh epazote is essential for chilpachole, green mole, tortilla soup, zucchini flowers, and quesillo quesadillas. The flavor is distinctive, and some dishes cannot be prepared authentically without it.

Bitter Orange
This rough-skinned citrus fruit is smaller than a classic orange. It is used for marinades to help eliminate strong odors and tenderize meats such as game and pork. Yucatán, Veracruz, Tabasco, and Chiapas appreciate the bitter orange's juice and use it in several dishes.

Corn

Fresh and dried corn have multiple uses in Mexican cooking. Hominy is used for pozole, dried corn for soups such as huachales or chacales, masa harina for tamales and tortillas, and fresh corn for grilling and boiling.

Garlic and White Onion

Both of these aromatic ingredients form the base for many sauces, soups, recados, and stews.

Jícama

Jícama is a globe-shaped turnip or edible root native to Mexico. Its golden-brown skin covers a starchy white interior. It is used raw in salads and eaten as a snack with chili powder and lime. The flavor is somewhat sweet, and it has a crunchy texture. It serves as an acceptable ingredient for vegan picadillo tacos, as it is suitable for sautéing.

Limas

Limas should not be confused with limes. This citrus fruit is double or triple the size of a lime and has a yellowish color. The flesh is light yellow and not as juicy as lime. The flavor is between sweet and bitter—more aromatic and less acid than lime. Typically used in Yucatecan cuisine and for desserts and cock-tails, lima is also a classic for Las Posadas. This citrus fruit is added to piñatas, among other fruits and candy.

Limes

Limes are a staple in Mexican cuisine. They are used for curing meats, cooking raw seafood, enhancing soups, making beverages. They are also used in fruit and vegetable salads, desserts, and as an anti-browning agent for avocado and guacamole.

Mint

Mint is not only used for making tea. In Mexican cuisine, mint is added to everything from chicken soups and broths to desserts and fruit salads.

Nopales

It is common to find cactus in various dishes such as nopales salad, grilled cactus with cheese and salsa, egg and pork dishes, smoothies, and even nutritional supplements. There are many varieties of nopales, all indigenous to Mexico, which is why this ingredient is used regularly in many traditional recipes. A cookout isn't complete without tender grilled cactus.

Plantains

Plantains are a staple of Southern Mexican cuisine. They are cut into slices, fried, and used as a side dish for rice and eggs. When overripe, they are cooked, mashed, and made into tortillas, which can be stuffed with cheese or refried beans. In Puebla and Oaxaca, plantains are used for making mole.

Potatoes

Potatoes are typically served with chorizo. They are also an ingredient for meatless dishes such as tortitas de papa, quesadillas, and cheese-potato chowder.

Squash

Chayote and other squashes such as zucchini are prevalent in meatless main dishes, moles, soups and salads, and side dishes, and are often mixed with other vegetables, tomatoes, and poblano peppers.

Tomatillos

Tomatillos are known as the Mexican husk tomato, but they are not tomatoes. The plant is related to the gooseberry and Chinese lantern plant. The flavor is acidic, and it can be green or deep purple in appearance. This ingredient is essential for green salsa, salads, and stews. The husk helps reduce the gel-like content of nopales.

Tomatoes

Tomatoes are essential in Mexican cuisine. They are used for sauces, pico de gallo, and guacamole, among many other dishes. Roma and beefsteak are preferred.

Yerba Santa (Mexican Pepperleaf)

Yerba santa is a staple in Chiapan and Oaxacan cuisines. The heart-shape leaf can be as big as the palm of a hand. Many families grow the plant in their gardens and use it in tamales, soups, and mole. The taste is similar to anise, with herbal notes.

CHILES

Did you know chiles originated in Mexico? The Aztec and Maya civilizations cultivated chiles and included them in many dishes. They also used them to fumigate homes and cure illnesses. After Cristóbal Colón's arrival, chile cultivars spread across the world.

In Mexican cuisine, chiles are an essential component of many dishes. We use them fresh and dried depending on the flavor profile we want. For instance, dried chiles provide a smoky note and not all are spicy. Dried chiles are common in cooked sauces such as moles and adobos and used to make vinegar-based spicy sauces. In contrast, fresh chiles are essential for salsas, pico de gallo, and guacamole.

Here are the most popular chiles in Mexican cuisine:

Chile de árbol. Also known as bird's beak and rat's tail, these chiles are used fresh and dried. When fresh, these chiles are green, turning a deep red when dried. This chile is six times hotter than a jalapeño, at between 15,000 and 30,000 Scoville Heat Units. Chile de árbol is a typical ingredient in hot salsas for tacos and vinegar-based hot sauces such as the sauce for tortas ahogadas.

Chile guajillo. When fresh, these chiles are called mirasol, and they are the most popular chiles in Mexican cuisine. The name "guajillo" refers to a big pod. This crop originated in the Bajío region. Guajillos are mild dried chiles with a range from 2,500 to 5,000 on the Scoville scale. They have a smoky flavor characteristic of enchilada sauces and are typically used in dishes such as birria. Guajillos come in two sizes. The smaller is called "puya." This chile is spicier than regular mirasol and also comes dried.

Chile poblano. This mild but flavorful chile is used for making chiles en nogada and other Mexican dishes such as the classic rajas with corn. These chiles originated in Puebla. When dried, poblanos are also known as "chile ancho" or "chile mulato." The heat ranges from 1,000 to 2,000 Scoville Heat Units. Dried chile ancho is perfect for adobos.

Chipotle peppers. These peppers are dried jalapeños smoked for added flavor and are used in sauces and dishes such as tinga and albóndigas. Chipotles play an essential role in Puebla's cuisine. These dried peppers can come pickled in a sweet broth and are used as garnishes in cemitas. The heat level ranges from 2,500 to 8,000 Scoville Heat Units. Chipotles are also known as "meco" and "morita."

Jalapeño peppers. Also known as "cuaresmeños," these peppers originated in Xalapa, Veracruz; the name comes from the region's name. This pepper is one of the most popular worldwide. They are mildly hot, averaging around 5,000 Scoville Heat Units. Typically used raw for chopped salsas and guacamoles and in cooked sauces with either tomatoes or tomatillos, these peppers are also popular for pickling.

Depending on the region, there might be other chile species. For instance, in the South, güeros, chimborote, and habaneros are staples in Yucatecan and Chiapan cuisines. In the North, chiles pasado, perones, and chiltepines are part of the daily diet. Serrano peppers and chile bola (cascabel) are very popular among taquerías in Mexico City. Pasilla (chilaca) is the main ingredient in salsa borracha, and mulato and chilhuacle chiles are present in Oaxacan favorites such as mole negro.

Here are some ingredients commonly kept on hand in Mexican pantries so typical meals can be easily prepared.

Beans

There are over 70 endemic bean species cultivated in Mexico. Some favorites are pinto (flor de mayo), bayo, azufrado, canario, mayo, yorimuni, and different varieties of black beans. Canned beans are acceptable, but many households enjoy cooking dried beans using a either a traditional or an electric pressure cooker.

Achiote (Annatto) Paste

Achiote, or annatto, is used for coloring and seasoning. The seeds are used for flavored oils and pastes. This condiment is typical in Southern Mexican–inspired cuisine and is known as a main ingredient for cochinita pibil. However, Tabasco, Oaxaca, Campeche, and Chiapas also grow and consume this plant.

Chocolate

The Olmecs created chocolate and the Mayas perfected it, making it a sacred drink. Nowadays, chocolate is enjoyed mixed with milk and can include almonds and cinnamon. Chocolate is also used in moles and other savory dishes.

Cinnamon, Cloves, and Anise

Cinnamon is used in desserts, fruit compotes, drinks, syrups, savory sauces, and café de olla. Cloves are aromatic flower buds that add warmth and a spicy note to moles and syrups. Anise adds aroma and a distinctive flavor to baked goods and desserts.

Condensed and Evaporated Milk

Condensed and evaporated milk are essential ingredients for preparing flans, rice puddings, atoles, drinks, sweet tamales, cookies, cakes, milk candies, dulce de leche, and jamoncillos (Mexican fudge).

Corn Husks

Corn husks are the leaves that surround corn cobs. They are used green when making tender, sweet corn tamales and dried for classic tamales. Dried corn husks are moistened before use for easy wrapping and securing of the tamal.

Hominy

Hominy is the name of the white corn used for pozole. It is available canned or bagged.

Masa Harina

Masa harina is corn flour used for making tortillas, sopes, huaraches, picaditas, tlacoyos, memelas, and gorditas. Masa harina can be white or blue.

Peanuts

Peanuts are used as a thickener for sauces and moles. They are also used for beverages, as salad garnishes, and for classic desserts such as mazapanes.

Piloncillo and Panela

Piloncillo is raw sugar formed into a cone; panela is also raw sugar but formed into a disk. Both are used for café de olla, candied pumpkin, and syrups. They also have savory applications such as preserving pickled chipotles and soaking ancho chiles for stuffing.

Pumpkin Seeds

Pumpkin seeds are used for sauces and moles, but they are the main ingredient in classic cookies, such as tortitas de Santa Clara from Puebla, and sweets called pepitorias and palanquetas.

Rice

Long-grain rice is preferred for cooking Mexican-style rice. Rinsing the rice prior to cooking removes excess starch, which prevents the rice from becoming lumpy and gummy in texture. The only exception to this is when making arroz con leche and horchata; the rice doesn't need to be rinsed when making rice pudding and this delicious beverage.

Sesame Seeds

Sesame seeds are an important ingredient in hot sauces such as salsa macha and moles. They are also used in fruity salads and as an accent for nutty flavors in baked goods.

Spices

Cumin, marjoram, bay leaves, and freshly ground black pepper are common seasonings for pork, fish, and other meats. They are also used for pickling and making enchilada sauces. Mexican oregano is stronger than Italian and is typically used in pozole.

OTHER INGREDIENTS

Along with the previously listed ingredients, here are some other items usually found in Mexican home kitchens.

Tortillas (Corn and Flour)

Corn and flour tortillas are essential in Mexican cooking. You may want to have different sizes: small street-taco and classic corn tortillas. For flour tortillas, use large for burritos, medium for tacos, and the smaller, thicker version for quesadillas. If not cooking your own, look for tortillas that are similar to homemade. Certain brands offer raw flour tortillas ready to cook on a comal. For corn tortillas, one option is to mix flour and corn masa flour. Or use nixtamalized corn flour for a softer texture tortilla. Storing tortillas is easy: Use a plastic container with a lid and keep them refrigerated.

Lard

Pork lard is very common in Mexican cuisine. It is needed for sautéing and quick-frying. Lard is also used for tamales, refried beans, and cookies (polvorones and hojarascas). Lard can be purchased, but you can also reserve bacon fat after cooking and store it in the refrigerator.

Fresh Chorizo

Mexican chorizo differs from Spanish. Depending on the region, chorizo can have different colors and textures. The most common is from Sinaloa and Sonora. It is made with pork and doesn't come in a casing but is crumbled and typically seasoned with chile colorado, vinegar, and spices. Chorizo is consumed in antojitos, combined with potatoes, served for breakfast with eggs, used for topping molletes, added to quesadillas, and used for queso fundido. If you can't find it locally, make your own. It is super easy to prepare and freezes well.

Mexican Crema

Mexican crema is sweet and resembles French crème fraîche. You can find it in many supermarkets in the dairy aisle alongside queso fresco and other dairy products from Latin America.

Queso Cotija

This cheese originated in Michoacán. It is made with raw milk, covered in a peppery red sauce, and matured for at least three months. It has a robust, salty taste with a refined aroma and is intended for crumbling and topping Mexican antojitos, such as flautas, sopes, enchiladas, tostadas, soups, and more.

Queso Fresco

Queso fresco is a young cheese. It is firm but with a soft texture and creamy flavor. Queso fresco can be shredded, crumbled, and even fried. It is used in stuffed chiles, quesadillas, and sopa de queso.

Queso Oaxaca

Queso Oaxaca is also called quesillo. It is made with raw milk and stretched into long strings that are then formed into a ball. Real quesillo is an artisanal cheese, but it can be found in the United States. This cheese melts easily and is creamy and mild, perfect for quesadillas and other antojitos such as memelas.

Queso Chihuahua

Queso Chihuahua is made by the Mennonite community using pasteurized milk. It is light yellow and has a mature but not excessively strong flavor, rather like a mild cheddar. This cheese is perfect for casseroles (pastel Azteca), cheesy enchiladas, chiles rellenos, queso fundido, and dishes that require a higher fat cheese and higher melting point. This cheese is widely available and typically comes shredded and bagged.

USEFUL EQUIPMENT

Cooking Mexican dishes at home requires a few gadgets and utensils that will make your life easier and set you up for making successful dishes.

PRESSURE COOKER

A pressure cooker saves time and helps achieve the best results when cooking beef, pork, chicken stock, soups, dried beans, tamales, and birria. An alternative to a classic stovetop pressure cooker is the Instant Pot.

COMAL

This flat griddle is used for many purposes, not only for cooking tortillas. A comal is great for roasting peppers, tomatoes, and garlic for salsas and for cooking gorditas, molotes, and sopes. If you do not have a comal, just use a nonstick skillet.

MOLCAJETE

The molcajete is a stone mortar used for mashing. Using a molcajete provides authenticity to a hot sauce. However, if you do not have one, use a blender or food processor.

CLAY POT

Mexican clay pots are not only pretty but cook wonderful frijoles de olla and caldos. They also are wonderful for making homemade yogurt and for resting bread dough. Clay pots are traditional but can be replaced with a cast-iron Dutch oven or pressure cooker.

TAMALERA

A tamalera is a huge pot that has a rack in the bottom for steaming, plus a lid. I prefer to use an Instant Pot or a medium steamer for cooking smaller batches of tamales. However, if you are cooking tamales for a crowd, a tamalera is very handy.

TORTILLA PRESS

Primarily for making corn tortillas, this press has other uses as well, such as helping make conchas and quesadillas. The heavy metal press is the perfect size for a medium corn tortilla. If you are planning to make your own tortillas, this is a recommended investment. Unfortunately, there is not a good substitute for this item.

INGREDIENT PREP

Mexican cuisine is all about developing flavors. One of the most important techniques is roasting ingredients, which, in Spanish, is known as *tatemar*. Tatemar means roasting ingredients almost to the point of getting burnt. For example, when making hot sauce, the tomatoes, chiles, garlic, and onion are roasted over direct fire until blistered, which develops the unique, smoky flavor characteristic of Mexican cuisine.

ROASTING VEGETABLES

The tatemado is done over a direct flame on a grill or on the stove. Using tongs, turn the vegetables until they are uniformly roasted all over. A comal is recommended for the tatemado of tomatoes, tomatillos, and garlic, although you can oven roast them at a high temperature. Poblano peppers should be roasted until blistered for easy peeling.

Garlic
Roast garlic cloves on a comal or griddle over medium heat for 2 to 3 minutes on each side, or until showing brown spots. If you roast with the skin on (which is acceptable), the flavor won't be as smoky.

Onions

Oven-roast onions at 400°F for 15 to 20 minutes. Whole onions should be brushed with oil and wrapped in aluminum foil; they may also be cut into chunks and spread out on a baking sheet. Or use a comal over medium heat, turning the onions with tongs.

Poblanos

The best way to blister poblanos is over a direct flame, turning them several times until completely roasted. Then, bag and wrap the roasted peppers with a cloth to create enough steam to peel the skin. Or deep-fry the poblanos at 275°F for 5 to 7 minutes, until the skin puffs and peels. You can also oven-roast the poblanos in a pan at 400°F for 7 minutes on each side. Remove the roasted peppers from the heat and cover them with foil to create steam, which will help the skin peel off easily.

Tomatillos and Tomatoes

These are traditionally roasted on a comal over medium heat, turning them occasionally, until they show brown spots. Another option is to halve and oven-roast them, then put them on a baking sheet and grill at 400°F for 7 to 10 minutes. Set them aside to rest for 10 minutes. Unlike tomatillos, tomatoes need to be peeled for a smoother texture in salsas and purees.

TOASTING DRIED CHILES

Some recipes call for toasting or frying dried chiles. This is done quickly to avoid the bitterness that can develop if they are toasted or fried for a long time or at a very high temperature. Another technique to develop flavors is toasting spices, nuts, and seeds.

Dried Peppers

Toast dried peppers in a skillet or comal over medium heat for no more than 1 minute, using tongs or a spatula to continuously move them to avoid burning. They are ready when the aroma is smoky and they show brown spots.

Dried Chiles

Toast dried chiles in a skillet over medium heat with 1 tablespoon of cooking oil for no more than 1 minute, using tongs or a spatula to continuously move them to avoid burning. They are ready when the aroma is smoky and they show brown spots.

Herbs, Spices, Nuts, and Seeds

Toast these in a skillet over medium heat for no more than 2 minutes. Some herbs, such as oregano or bay leaves, burn fast, so make sure to stir them continuously to achieve even toasting.

ABOUT THE RECIPES

In this cookbook, you will find Mexican home-cooking recipes that use easy to find ingredients. These recipes, which I grew up with, represent many different regions across Mexico.

All the recipes include the name in both Spanish and English. You will see the recipe's origin at the top, as well as labels indicating whether it takes 30 minutes or less to make or is vegetarian or vegan. You'll also see if you need any special equipment for that particular recipe. Plus, there are plenty of tips with ingredient substitutions, advice on avoiding problems, and expert recommendations to ensure home-cooking success.

I hope you enjoy my collection of homestyle recipes and that, by going through these pages, you get inspired to try one or several of these wonderful Mexican dishes that you've never tasted before. Let's cook!

STAPLES

TORTILLAS DE MAÍZ CASERAS
HOMEMADE CORN TORTILLAS

Origin: Mexico | Vegan | Prep time: 30 minutes, plus 2 hours to rest | Cook time: 3 minutes each | Makes 12 tortillas | Special equipment: cast-iron skillet or griddle, tortilla press

Tortillas date to pre-Columbian times and are a quintessential companion to any Mexican meal. Tortillas come in different sizes and colors. The classic recipe uses nixtamalized corn flour (not cornmeal), which can be white, yellow, or blue, depending on the masa harina. The addition of guajillo sauce results in red tortillas and cilantro nopal paste produces a green version. Don't let the prep time intimidate you! It's almost all hands-off time while the masa harina hydrates. Not covering and resting the dough for long enough could result in brittle, dry tortillas.

2 cups masa harina

½ teaspoon sea salt

1 cup plus ⅔ cup hot water, plus more if needed (see tip)

1. Combine the masa harina and salt in a medium bowl and use your hands to mix them together.

2. Add the warm water slowly to start hydrating the masa. Work the dough with your hands until it feels like Play-Doh, not watery or runny. Continue mixing for 10 minutes, until the dough feels soft and holds together smoothly when a small amount is pressed.

3. Form the dough into a ball and wrap it in plastic wrap. Let sit on the counter for 2 hours.

4. While the dough rests, make the plastic squares for the tortilla press. Using scissors, cut off the sealing portion of a gallon freezer bag (the plastic is thicker), and cut down both sides to open the bag completely into two plastic squares.

5. Unwrap the dough and work it with your hands again. If the dough feels dry, moisten your hands with water and continue working it until it feels soft and doesn't stick to your hands.

6. Form 12 balls, each the size of the palm of your hand. (For smaller tortillas, use less dough.) Place the balls in a medium bowl and cover them with a damp cloth; masa harina dough dries fast and needs to stay moist.

7. Preheat a cast-iron skillet or griddle over medium heat (if the heat is too high, it could burn the tortillas).

8. Open the tortilla press and lay out one of the plastic squares. Place one dough ball on top of the plastic square and cover it with the second plastic square. Clamp down the tortilla press and press gently.

9. Remove the tortilla from the press and carefully peel off the plastic. Cook the tortilla in the skillet for 30 seconds, until the edges are semi-cooked. Flip immediately and cook for 1½ minutes. When little bubbles form on top of the tortilla, flip it again. Press the center; if the tortilla puffs up, it is done cooking. Wrap the cooked tortilla in a cloth and transfer it to a tortilla warmer. Repeat with the remaining dough.

TIP

The amount of water required depends on the coarseness of the masa harina. Add water incrementally to avoid adding too much. The water should be hot but not to the point that it burns. To avoid hard, dry tortillas, the masa harina needs to rest for at least 2 hours. The best tortillas are those that puff while cooking. If your tortillas do not puff at first, try again! Practice makes perfect, so don't get discouraged. You'll soon become an expert.

Masa harina stores well wrapped in plastic and refrigerated in a lidded container, so it can be mixed in advance. Moisten your hands with water and rework the masa until it is soft but not sticky before making the tortillas. Cooked cold tortillas can be stored in a plastic bag in the refrigerator for up to 2 days. To reheat day-old tortillas, wet them with water and heat them on the griddle.

VARIATION

Try making blue corn tortillas. The process is the same as described, except you use blue masa harina and 2 cups of water as blue masa harina tends to be coarser.

TORTILLAS DE HARINA AL ESTILO CHIHUAHUA
CHIHUAHUA-STYLE FLOUR TORTILLAS

Origin: Chihuahua | Vegan | Prep time: 20 minutes, plus 1 hour to rest | Cook time: 5 minutes each | Makes 12 tortillas | Special equipment: cast-iron skillet

This recipe is from my Aunt Julieta's recipe box. These flour tortillas are thicker and smaller than those made in other Northern Mexican states. Flour tortillas are a kitchen staple in Chihuahua. Every evening, tortillas are freshly made to pair with homestyle classics such as caldillo de res and chile con queso. This same recipe works for sopaipillas and empanadas. Using the correct measurements, resting the dough, and keeping it moist are key to successful flour tortillas.

2½ cups all-purpose flour, sifted

1 teaspoon salt

1 teaspoon baking powder

½ cup vegetable shortening, at room temperature, plus a dab for kneading

1 cup hot water (see tip)

1. Combine the flour, salt, and baking powder in a medium bowl and mix well. Using your hands or a stand mixer, incorporate the shortening until the texture is like sand.

2. Add the water, a little bit at a time, and knead the dough for 5 to 8 minutes, until moist and soft but not sticky.

3. Form the dough into a ball. Take a dab of shortening and massage the dough with it. Place the dough ball in a lidded container and cover it with plastic wrap. Let it rest for 1 hour on the counter.

4. Divide the dough into 12 balls. Cover the balls with a cloth to prevent them drying out.

5. Sprinkle some flour on a work surface and, using a floured rolling pin, roll one dough ball into a thick 8-inch circle. Flip and turn the dough to achieve the rounded form. Do not get discouraged if the tortilla is not perfectly round. Sprinkle the tortilla with flour and set aside. Repeat with the remaining dough.

6. Preheat a cast-iron skillet over medium heat. Cook the tortilla for 30 seconds. When bubbles form, flip the tortilla and press it with a spatula, grill press, steak weight, or double-folded thick towel. You will see the tortilla start to puff, which is normal. When golden-brown spots are visible on both sides, the tortilla is ready. Try not to overcook them.

TIP

It is essential to rest the dough to get that characteristic flaky, buttery texture. The water should be hot but not to the point that it burns. The shortening and plastic wrap help keep the dough moist. Otherwise, it will form a crust and the tortilla won't cook as expected. A thick cast-iron skillet will produce better results. Making flour tortillas requires time and practice. The more you make them, the more expert you will become.

FOODS ASSOCIATED WITH CONVENTS

After the Spanish conquest, the viceroy in Puebla represented the King of Spain in the territory. This government had members of the King's court, as well as Spanish missionaries and nuns. The nuns played a key role in celebrations and catering government events. The most famous nuns were from Convento de Santa Rosa (birthplace of mole poblano). Augustinian Recollect nuns from the Santa Monica convent invented chiles en nogada. The sisters from the Santa Clara convent were experts in sweets and baking. They invented tortitas de Santa Clara (homemade cookies made with pepitas) and rompope (a Mexican version of eggnog). The nuns cleverly used local ingredients with Spanish condiments, creating intricate flavors and a new cuisine. The best examples are tinga poblana and chiles en nogada. Other culinary treasures created by nuns include enchiladas and chilaquiles. The first recipe book from the Virreinal era is attributed to Sor Juana Inés de la Cruz, a nun from the order of Barefoot Carmelites of Mexico and the first poet in Hispanic America.

SALSA DE PICO DE GALLO
PICO DE GALLO SALSA

Origin: Mexico | 30 Minutes or Less, Vegan | Prep time: 20 minutes | Makes 2 cups

Pico de gallo salsa is also called salsa Mexicana or salsa fresca. The name, which means "rooster's beak," perhaps came about because salsa was initially eaten by pinching it between the thumb and finger, making the shape of a beak. True or not, this salsa is a staple in home cooking. At my mom's table, a good salsa Mexicana and guacamole were regular garnishes. We use this for garnishing soups and broths; in rice, tacos, tostadas, and quesadillas; on top of molletes; to cook huevos a la Mexicana; and much more.

½ small white onion, diced

1 large jalapeño pepper, seeded, deveined, and finely chopped

2 large Roma tomatoes, diced

½ teaspoon salt

Juice of ½ lime

¼ cup cilantro leaves, chopped

In a medium mixing bowl, combine the onion, jalapeño, and tomatoes. Mix well. Season with the salt and lime juice. Stir and top with the cilantro before serving in a classic salsa bowl.

TIP
Using the freshest ingredients is vital for the best pico de gallo. Choose ripe tomatoes with firm flesh and opt for Roma tomatoes, if possible. There should be more tomato than onion. Cilantro is best when roughly chopped or torn with your hands. Store pico de gallo in an airtight container in the refrigerator for up to 3 days. If storing, omit the cilantro until just before serving.

VARIATION
For a spicier pico de gallo, substitute the jalapeño with 1 or 2 serrano peppers. The Roma tomatoes could also be replaced with 1 beefsteak tomato or 2 tomatoes on the vine.

SALSA VERDE PICANTE CON CHILE DE ÁRBOL FRESCO

SPICY TOMATILLO SALSA WITH FRESH CHILE DE ÁRBOL

Origin: Estado de Mexico, Tlaxcala, Mexico City, Oaxaca, Puebla, Hidalgo, Michoacán, and Morelos | 30 Minutes or Less, Vegan | Prep time: 10 minutes | Cook time: 2 minutes
Makes 2 cups | Special equipment: comal or griddle, molcajete or blender

Salsa verde dates back to the Aztec Empire. The base of the sauce is tomatillos, also called Mexican husk tomato or miltomate. Salsa verde can be raw or cooked. Typically, the cooked sauce is for stews and enchiladas and the raw is appropriate for garnishing almost everything. Each state prepares salsa verde with its own unique touch. For example, in Tlaxcala and Puebla, salsa could include pápaloquelite, a pungent Mexican herb. This recipe is inspired by the Oaxacan version, which has a spicy and herbaceous flavor.

8 medium tomatillos, husked and cleaned

3 fresh chile de árbol peppers, stemmed

1 garlic clove

½ teaspoon coarse salt

1 tablespoon water (optional)

⅓ red onion, finely chopped

½ cup cilantro leaves, torn

1. Place a comal or griddle on the stovetop over medium heat. When it is hot, blister the tomatillos for less than 1 minute. The tomatillos must remain raw but show some blistering. Do the same with the chiles and garlic. The blistering or tatemado of the ingredients helps develop the smoky flavor characteristic of Mexican sauces. For creating a more authentic salsa verde, do not skip this step.

2. If using a molcajete, mash the garlic with the salt, then add the peppers and mash again. Finally, add the tomatillos, one at a time, and continue mashing until a chunky salsa forms. If using a blender, combine the peppers, garlic, salt, and water. Pulse to achieve a chunky salsa texture. Try not to use more water.

3. Stir in the onion. Taste and adjust with more salt as needed. Top with the cilantro immediately before serving.

SALSA DE JALAPEÑO ROJO
RED JALAPEÑO SALSA

Origin: Mexico | 30 Minutes or Less, Vegan | Prep time: 5 minutes | Cook time: 20 minutes
Makes 2 cups | Special equipment: comal or griddle, blender

Enrique Olvera—recipient of 6 Michelin Stars and the most awarded Mexican chef—once said that embracing his roots, reinventing his mom's recipes, and using Mexican indigenous techniques such as "burning" the ingredients changed his life. So, I say, do not be afraid of going back to your roots; it could be a life-changer.

2 large or 3 small Roma tomatoes

3 red jalapeño peppers

2 garlic cloves

½ teaspoon coarse salt

1. Place a comal or griddle on the stovetop over high heat. When it is hot, roast the tomatoes and jalapeños for 10 to 15 minutes, until fully blistered and showing brown marks.

2. Roast the garlic for 2 to 3 minutes, until golden brown.

3. For a smoother salsa, remove the tomato skins before blending.

4. Combine the tomatoes, jalapeños, and garlic in a blender and blend to a smooth consistency. Season with the salt.

TIP

Choose the spiciness of your salsa by adding more or fewer jalapeño peppers. Do not worry if the garlic turns brown; the flavor is better when toasted. As with other spicy sauces, the tatemado, or roasting of the vegetables, is essential for creating the smoky notes that make a Mexican salsa authentic. If you cannot find red jalapeño peppers, buy them green and let them mature in a sunny window or use green jalapeños for a milder taste.

SALSA PICANTE DE CHILE DE ÁRBOL

CHILE DE ÁRBOL HOT SAUCE

Origin: Jalisco | 30 Minutes or Less, Vegan | Prep time: 20 minutes | Makes 2 cups | Special equipment: blender

Also called salsa tapatía, this hot sauce is the quintessential ingredient in the popular tortas ahogadas. However, it is widely used to drizzle on chicharróns, potato chips, soups, crudites, and almost everything.

1 cup dried chile de árbol, stemmed

2 cups boiling water

2 garlic cloves

2 tablespoons apple cider vinegar

1 teaspoon ground cumin

1 teaspoon dried marjoram

1 tablespoon salt

2 tablespoons toasted sesame seeds

1. Soak the chiles in the water for 10 to 15 minutes. Reserve 1 cup of the chile soaking water for blending.

2. Pour the reserved soaking water into a blender and add the chiles, garlic, vinegar, cumin, marjoram, salt, and sesame seeds.

3. Blend on high and pour into a sauce bottle for later use.

TIP

Buy small sauce bottles and fill them with this sauce. They make wonderful gifts.

SALSA DE CHILE HABANERO Y TOMATE
HABANERO-TOMATO SALSA

Origin: Yucatán | 30 Minutes or Less, Vegan | Prep time: 5 minutes, plus 15 minutes to rest | Makes 2 cups

Habanero, onion, and tomatoes come together in a fresh chopped salsa classic that is perfect for garnishing Yucatecan sopa de lima. But this salsa also pairs wonderfully with other antojitos such as carnitas tacos and grilled chicken or beef. In Mexican cuisine, fresh garnishes and salsas play a significant role in adding texture and layering flavors, elevating dishes to another level of yumminess.

2 Roma tomatoes, diced

⅓ red onion, diced

1 habanero, chopped

⅓ cup fresh cilantro leaves

¼ cup bitter orange juice

1 teaspoon sea salt

Combine the tomatoes, onion, habanero, and cilantro in a medium bowl. Stir and season with the bitter orange juice and salt. Stir again and allow the salsa to marinate for 15 minutes before serving. Keep the salsa refrigerated in an airtight container until ready to use.

VARIATION

Replace the red onion with white onion and the bitter orange with ¼ cup of orange juice mixed with 1 tablespoon of apple cider vinegar.

GUACAMOLE DE AGUACATE ASADO
GRILLED GUACAMOLE

Origin: Mexico | 30 Minutes or Less, Vegan | Prep time: 15 minutes | Cook time: 10 minutes
Makes 1½ cups | Special equipment: charcoal grill or skillet, molcajete or blender

Avocado is found throughout Mexican cuisine. It's used in many ways, and grilling it gives it a nice smoky flavor that complements the guacamole mix. Guacamole typically has tomato, onion, jalapeño, lime juice, and cilantro, but there are a few variations and this is one of them. This guacamole is the perfect companion to carnitas, chicharróns, and corn chips, and it is ideal for making guacamole tacos.

1 avocado

¼ teaspoon corn oil (or vegetable or grapeseed oil)

1 garlic clove

1 serrano pepper (optional)

½ teaspoon coarse salt

1 teaspoon water (optional)

Juice of 1 lime

⅓ cup roughly chopped cilantro

1. Light a charcoal grill or heat a skillet over high heat.

2. Wash the avocado with soap and water. Dry it with a paper towel and cut it in half. Remove the pit and brush the cut surfaces with the oil.

3. Lower the heat to medium and grill the avocado, cut-side down, for 5 to 7 minutes, or until grill marks appear. Set it aside.

4. In the same skillet, roast the garlic and serrano pepper (if using) in the skillet. When golden brown or blistered, remove them from heat and mash in a molcajete. Add the salt and continue mashing. If you do not have a molcajete, blend the ingredients in a blender with the water.

5. Scoop out the grilled avocado and mash it with the garlic-serrano mixture. When all is incorporated, add the lime juice and mix again.

6. Top the guacamole with the cilantro and enjoy with corn chips, tacos, carnitas, and much more.

TIP

Lime juice prevents the avocado from browning, so do not leave it out. A charcoal grill provides a more authentic flavor, but a skillet on the stovetop works fine. Use a high smoke point oil such as corn, vegetable, or grapeseed.

SALSA MACHA
DRIED CHILE OIL SAUCE

Origin: Michoacán, Oaxaca, and Veracruz | Vegan | Prep time: 10 minutes | Cook time: 10 minutes, plus 20 minutes to steep | Makes 1 cup | Special equipment: food processor

There are a few versions and different ways of making this dried chile oil sauce. In Orizaba, chipotle peppers are used; in Michoacán, they use chiles de árbol; and in Oaxaca, anchos, guajillos, and chipotles are used. The oil turns red and is commonly used for cooking or garnishing caldos. It is important to use an oil with a high smoke point to avoid the oil burning and altering the taste. My method of frying the dried peppers first allows for a successful result.

1 cup stemmed and seeded dried chile de árbol (keep the seeds for spicier version)

½ cup corn, vegetable, or grapeseed oil

2 garlic cloves, finely chopped

3 tablespoons sesame seeds

1 teaspoon coarse sea salt

1. In a food processor, process the chile de árbol into flakes. Some like the flakes bigger and others smaller. Crush depending on your taste.

2. Heat the oil in a small saucepan over high heat. When the oil is bubbling, carefully remove the pan from the heat and set on a firm surface. The oil will be scalding, so please exercise caution.

3. Carefully add the pepper flakes, garlic, and sesame seeds.

4. Return the saucepan to the stove over low heat and simmer for 5 to 7 minutes. Then, remove the saucepan from the heat, add the salt, and stir. Let the ingredients steep for about 20 minutes, until the oil is at room temperature.

5. The oil will turn red, and the ingredients will be toasty. Pour the salsa macha into a mason jar with a lid and store it in the pantry.

TIP

If you prefer to make salsa macha the traditional way by frying the dried chiles, please do. The only recommendation is to avoid frying them too long, as dried peppers burn fast and become bitter.

CEBOLLITAS MORADAS EN ESCABECHE
PICKLED RED ONIONS

Origin: Yucatán | Vegan | Prep time: 15 minutes, plus 30 minutes to marinate
Makes 2 cups

In Mexican cuisine, we like to garnish our dishes with pickled onions. In fact, it's unthinkable to eat classic tortas ahogadas or pibil dishes without including pickled onions on the side. Pickled onions add texture and balance the flavors in many dishes, thanks to the vinegar and citrus notes. These onions can also be mixed with chopped habanero or serrano peppers.

1 cup warm water

⅓ cup white vinegar

Juice of 1 lime

1 teaspoon coarse salt

½ teaspoon freshly ground black pepper

½ teaspoon Mexican oregano

1 red onion, thinly sliced

In a large bowl, combine the water, vinegar, lime juice, and salt. Stir for 5 minutes to dissolve the salt, then stir in the black pepper, oregano, and onion. Stir until combined, then set it aside to marinate for 30 minutes, or until the mixture turns pink. Serve or store in a mason jar in the refrigerator.

BREAKFAST

HUEVOS RANCHEROS
RANCHERO EGGS

Origin: Mexico | 30 Minutes or Less, Vegetarian | Prep time: 15 minutes
Cook time: 15 minutes | Serves 2

Huevos rancheros are two sunny-side-up eggs served over fried tortillas and covered with a tomatoey hot sauce. The dish is paired with refried beans, freshly made bolillo toast with butter, a cup of coffee, and orange juice. This breakfast is very popular in Mexico and a traditional way to start the day on the right foot. In Spanish, we say, "barriga llena corazón contento," which means "full belly and a happy heart."

½ cup Red Jalapeño Salsa (page 28)

1 cup Mayocoba Refried Beans (page 111)

4 tablespoons cooking oil

4 corn tortillas, divided

4 farm-fresh eggs, at room temperature, divided

Nonstick cooking spray

1 teaspoon water

2 halved, toasted, and buttered bolillos

1. In a small saucepan over medium heat, warm the salsa.

2. In the microwave or another small saucepan, heat the refried beans.

3. Heat the oil in a skillet over medium-high heat. Quickly fry 2 tortillas, taking care not to let them get crispy, and set them on a paper towel–lined plate to absorb any extra fat. Then, transfer the tortillas to a serving plate and set it aside.

4. Crack 2 eggs into a small bowl, trying to keep the yolks intact.

5. Wipe out the skillet and spray it with cooking spray, then place it over low heat. Pour the eggs carefully into the skillet. Add the water, cover with a lid, and cook for 2 minutes, or until the whites are set and the yolks look a bit runny. The longer you leave the lid on, the more the yolk will cook. If you prefer over-easy or cooked yolks, cook for 3 minutes or more.

6. Slide the eggs on top of the tortillas. Repeat with the remaining eggs and tortillas.

7. Cover the eggs with the salsa and serve with the refried beans and buttery toasted bolillos.

TIP

Using room temperature eggs keeps them from overcooking. Make sure to take the eggs out of the refrigerator 20 minutes before cooking them. Using fresh eggs also creates a nicer looking sunny-side up with a tighter white.

HUEVOS DIVORCIADOS
DIVORCED EGGS

Origin: Mexico | 30 Minutes or Less, Vegetarian | Prep time: 15 minutes
Cook time: 15 minutes | Serves 2

Divorced eggs are similar to ranchero eggs, except they lack the fried tortilla and the eggs are covered with different sauces and separated by refried beans or chilaquiles. This fun dish is typically served on weekends in many Mexico City households.

½ cup Spicy Tomatillo Salsa with Fresh Chile de Árbol (page 27)

½ cup Red Jalapeño Salsa (page 28)

1 cup Mayocoba Refried Beans (page 111)

4 fresh eggs, at room temperature, divided

Nonstick cooking spray

1. Heat the tomatillo salsa and the red salsa in separate saucepans over medium heat or in separate bowls in the microwave.

2. Reheat the refried beans in a skillet over medium heat or in the microwave.

3. Crack 2 eggs into a ramekin.

4. Spray a separate skillet twice with cooking spray and set it over medium heat. Warm the skillet, but make sure it is not scorching hot.

5. Pour the eggs carefully into the skillet. Cover with a lid and cook for 2 minutes, or until the whites are set and the yolks look a bit runny. The longer you leave the lid on, the more the yolk will cook. If you prefer over-easy or cooked yolks, cook for 3 minutes or more.

6. Repeat with the remaining eggs.

7. To serve, slide the eggs onto a plate. Cover one egg with warm red salsa and the other with warm tomatillo salsa. Between them, add the beans.

TIP

Prepare the sauces and the beans the day before to save time, especially if you are cooking for four or more people. When cooking the eggs, you can use 1 teaspoon of water instead of the oil spray.

CHILAQUILES VERDES
GREEN CHILAQUILES

Origin: Mexico | Prep time: 30 minutes | Cook time: 30 minutes | Serves 4
Special equipment: comal, blender

There is no clear history on the origins of chilaquiles, but the name comes from the Náhuatl *chilaquili—chil* (chile) and *aquili* (for submerging in chili sauce). This dish is a typical breakfast item in many Mexican households. It is economical and can be served red, green, or with mole sauce. Shredded chicken is a common addition, as is serving them alongside eggs and refried beans. For an authentic presentation, top them with onion, Mexican crema, and ranchero cheese.

For the green tomatillo salsa

10 fresh tomatillos, husked and washed, or 1 (16-ounce) can cooked tomatillos, drained

2 or 3 serrano peppers, or 2 jalapeños for less heat

2 garlic cloves

⅓ cup cilantro leaves

1 tablespoon chicken bouillon

Salt (optional)

For the chilaquiles

1 cup high smoke point oil, such as corn, vegetable, or grapeseed oil

8 corn tortillas, cut into triangles

½ cup shredded chicken

½ cup crumbled Ranchero queso fresco or cotija cheese

¼ onion, cut into rounds

½ cup Mexican crema

To make the green tomatillo salsa

1. Place the tomatillos in a large saucepan, add water to cover, and set it over medium heat. Bring to a simmer for 10 to 15 minutes, or until the tomatillos turn yellow-green. To avoid bitterness, do not use high heat or overcook. Turn off the heat and leave the tomatillos in the warm water for about 10 minutes. Remove them from the water and set them aside to cool, reserving ½ cup of the cooking water. Tomatillos need to be cold before blending to avoid developing bitterness.

2. In a comal, roast the serrano peppers with the garlic.

3. Transfer the tomatillos to a blender with the peppers, garlic, and cilantro. Add the reserved cooking water and blend until smooth. It should not be watery.

4. In a saucepan over medium heat, pour in the tomatillo salsa and chicken bouillon and simmer for 15 minutes. Taste and add salt (if using) or more water if necessary. Turn off the heat and keep the sauce covered with a lid until ready to use.

To make the chilaquiles

5. Heat the oil in a deep saucepan or cast-iron skillet over high heat. When the oil starts bubbling, add the tortilla triangles, one handful at a time. Do not overcrowd the pan and take care to avoid burns.

6. When the chips are golden brown, transfer them to a paper towel–lined plate to remove excess fat. Repeat until all tortilla chips are fried, then set aside.

7. Drown a handful of chips in the warm salsa for 1 or 2 seconds only (they need to stay crispy).

8. Place the drowned chips onto four plates and add the chicken. Drizzle each with additional sauce.

9. Top each plate with queso fresco, two onion slices, and Mexican crema.

TIP

Use yellow corn tortillas. Preferably, after cutting them, leave them on a tray to dry overnight for crispier chips that absorb less oil. Commercial corn chips absorb too much sauce and do not work well. These chilaquiles taste great with Mayocoba Re-fried Beans (page 111) and sunny-side-up eggs.

MACHACA CON HUEVO
BEEF MACHACA WITH EGGS

Origin: Sonora and Nuevo León | Prep time: 15 minutes | Cook time: 30 minutes | Serves 4

Machaca is dried skirt steak smashed in a pestle. If you can't find it at the supermarket, you can use beef jerky, grilled and ground with garlic in a molcajete or food processor. Beef machaca is a staple from Sonora and Nuevo Leon. Usually, the meat is seasoned with salt and dried in the sun for several days. The taste is a bit salty but delicious.

1 tablespoon corn oil

1½ cups machaca

1 cup finely chopped white onion

1 large garlic clove, finely chopped

1 jalapeño pepper or 2 serrano peppers, finely chopped

2 cups diced beefsteak tomatoes

Salt (optional)

Freshly ground black pepper

8 eggs

8 Chihuahua-Style Flour Tortillas (page 24)

Dried Chile Oil Sauce (page 32)

1. In a large skillet over medium heat, warm the oil. Add the machaca and sauté for 5 to 7 minutes, stirring constantly. Add the onion and garlic and sauté for another 5 minutes, stirring. Add the jalapeño and cook for 2 minutes. Stir in the tomatoes and simmer for another 5 minutes to allow the tomatoes to release the juices.

2. Taste and season with salt (if using) and black pepper.

3. Crack the eggs into a large bowl and mix with a whisk. Add the eggs to the machaca and stir to combine. Lower the heat and cook the eggs for 5 minutes (or less, if you prefer a softer egg consistency).

4. Serve with a side of tortillas and dried chile oil sauce.

TIP
Consider cooking your homemade machaca a day in advance. Cook 1 pound of skirt steak in the pressure cooker with 4 cups of water, 1 garlic clove, ½ onion, 1 teaspoon of marjoram, 1 tablespoon of beef bouillon, and 1 bay leaf. Shred and fry until crispy. If using commercial beef machaca, find one that is Mexican style. You can buy it on Amazon.

HUEVOS CON CHORIZO A LA MEXICANA

MEXICAN CHORIZO WITH EGGS

Origin: Mexico | Prep: 15 minutes | Cook time: 30 minutes | Serves 4

Mexican chorizo differs from the classic Spanish style in that it is made with uncooked pork, whereas the Spanish version is usually aged and smoked. Mexican chorizo looks like small crumbles of seasoned pork meat when fully cooked.

1 cup ground Homemade Pork Chorizo (page 104)

8 eggs

Pinch freshly ground black pepper

Pico de Gallo Salsa (page 26), for serving

4 Chihuahua-Style Flour Tortillas (page 24), for serving

1. In a skillet over medium heat, cook the chorizo for 20 minutes, or until all the fat has rendered. Remove the excess fat and make sure the chorizo is crispy, crumbly, and reddish brown.

2. Crack the eggs into a large bowl and mix them with a whisk. Sprinkle with the pepper and mix again. Add the eggs to the chorizo and cook for 7 minutes.

3. Serve with a side of pico de gallo and tortillas.

TIP

Mexican chorizo looks like a reddish paste with spices. It can come packaged in a square container or formed into small sausage-like links. If you prefer a vegetarian option, choose Mexican soy chorizo, which tastes very similar. Vegetarian chorizo takes about 45 minutes to brown.

TACOS DE HUEVO CON NOPALES
CACTUS AND EGG TACOS

Origin: Mexico | Vegetarian | Prep time: 15 minutes | Cook time: 30 minutes | Serves 4
Special equipment: comal or griddle

Nopal cactus is a common ingredient in many Mexican dishes. Nopales are part of the indigenous culinary legacy and a humble ingredient that now is considered a super-food. My mom served this to us as it is economical and filling. In the United States, it can be challenging to find fresh nopales, but the canned variety tastes similar and helps tame the craving for Mom's tasty breakfast.

6 eggs, at room temperature

1 tablespoon cooking oil

2 cups fresh or canned cactus nopales, diced and rinsed

½ white onion, finely chopped

1 serrano pepper, finely chopped (optional)

Salt

Freshly ground black pepper

Homemade Corn Tortillas (page 22), for serving

Spicy Tomatillo Salsa with Fresh Chile de Árbol (page 27), for serving

1. Crack the eggs into a medium bowl. Whisk and set aside.

2. Heat the oil in a skillet over medium heat. Add the nopales and sauté for 15 minutes, or until they turn dark green with some browning marks.

3. Stir in the onion and serrano pepper (if using) and cook for 5 minutes. Season with salt and black pepper.

4. Pour the eggs on top and stir them in. Cook the eggs for no longer than 7 minutes, then remove the skillet from the heat and set aside.

5. Warm the tortillas in a comal or griddle, then stuff each tortilla with the egg mixture. Garnish with salsa and serve.

TIP

If using canned nopales, choose those preserved in salted water, not the pickled cactus. There is no need to dice canned nopales as they come in strips. Trying to chop cooked cactus destroys it as it is tender. Canned nopales cook faster, so they cook in half the time.

MOLLETES CON FRIJOLES MAYOCOBA

TOAST WITH MAYOCOBA REFRIED BEANS AND CHEESE

Origin: Mexico | Vegetarian | Prep time: 15 minutes | Cook time: 20 minutes | Serves 2

No one is certain how the molletes with beans became a breakfast favorite in Mexico City. The word "mollete" is Spanish and refers to a type of bread. However, molletes come in different presentations throughout Latin America, and some are even sweet. This version is the one I grew up with at home.

2 bolillo breads or 2 small baguettes, halved

1 teaspoon butter or margarine, at room temperature

½ cup Mayocoba Refried Beans (page 111)

4 slices Chihuahua cheese or white Monterey Jack cheese

1 cup Pico de Gallo Salsa (page 26)

1. Preheat the oven to 375°F.
2. Remove some of the crust from the bread and spread each half with some butter.
3. Spread an equal amount of beans on each piece of bread and top it with the cheese.
4. Place the molletes on a baking sheet and bake for 20 minutes or more, depending on how toasty you like your bread.
5. Serve immediately with the salsa.

TIP

Use black or pinto beans if you do not have Mayocoba. Canned refried beans work, too.

HUEVOS AHOGADOS
DROWNED EGGS

Origin: Puebla | Prep time: 15 minutes | Cook time: 45 minutes | Serves 4
Special equipment: comal or griddle, blender

Drowned eggs are similar to eggs in purgatory or the Middle Eastern shakshuka, but in Mexico, we use a brothy sauce made with either guajillo chiles or serrano peppers and roasted tomatoes. The secret to success with this recipe is to break each egg into a ramekin before adding it to the sauce so the yolk doesn't break. Huevos ahogados is a typical brunch meal, and many families serve it during Lent for lunch.

5 guajillo chiles, stemmed, seeded, and rinsed

1 cup hot water

2 garlic cloves

½ white onion

8 Roma tomatoes

1 tablespoon cooking oil

1 teaspoon ground cumin

1 teaspoon ground Mexican oregano

1 tablespoon chicken bouillon

½ cup vegetable stock

Salt (optional)

8 eggs

½ cup diced queso fresco (firm texture, not for crumbling)

¼ cup cilantro leaves, for garnish

1. In a large bowl, soak the guajillo chiles in the hot water for 10 to 15 minutes, until soft. Reserve 1 cup of the chile soaking water.

2. Meanwhile, heat the comal or griddle over medium heat. Add the garlic and roast for 2 to 3 minutes. Add the onion and roast for 5 minutes. Add the tomatoes and roast for 10 to 15 minutes, until all the vegetables are blistered and browned. Transfer them to a plate, let them cool, and peel the tomatoes.

3. In a blender, combine the soaked peppers with the roasted vegetables. Add the reserved soaking water and blend until velvety.

4. In a deep sauté pan over medium heat, warm the oil and slowly pour the sauce in to avoid splattering. Season with the cumin, oregano, and bouillon. Mix well, add the vegetable stock, and let simmer for 15 minutes. Taste and add salt (if using).

5. When the sauce is bubbling, crack each egg, one at a time, into a ramekin and carefully add it to the sauce, along with the queso fresco. Once all the eggs have been added, cover the pan and poach for 8 minutes; if you prefer firmer yolks, cook for 2 minutes more.

6. Serve the eggs in a large bowl with some sauce and garnished with cilantro.

TIP

A firm queso fresco won't melt while cooking in the sauce. It is essential to use a deep sauté pan with a lid. Use a cast-iron, aluminum, or Mexican clay pot.

Pair this dish with beans, warm corn tortillas, or toasted bolillos.

BREAKFAST IN MEXICO

In Mexican households, breakfast is abundant. Dishes such as huevos rancheros or chilaquiles are staples, but pastries, natural juices, coffee, and nata never fail. In the North, machaca con huevo is preferred, whereas in the South, eggs are served with habanero sauces and plantains. Simple options such as molletes (a bolillo with refried beans and cheese), tortas de huevo, or tamales are popular with students and working people. Weekend breakfast means barbacoa, menudo, and caldos to cure the previous night's excesses. Breakfast is the perfect occasion to sit down with the family and chat. In Mexico, missing breakfast is omitting a vital part of the day, and Mexicans who have to skip breakfast will often find a way to sneak out of work to get some. Taquitos de huevo with cactus, quesadillas, enchiladas, and gorditas are popular options, as are fruit licuados, champurrado, and warm oatmeal. Mexico has the most delicious breakfast options, and there is no better breakfast than the one cooked with love in Mom's kitchen.

SNACKS AND APPETIZERS

TLACOYOS DE FRIJOL CON QUESO

CORN CAKES STUFFED WITH CHEESE AND BEANS

Origin: Hidalgo | Vegetarian | Prep time: 40 minutes | Cook time: 15 minutes | Serves 4
Special equipment: comal or cast-iron skillet

The name for these small, oval, bean-filled corn cakes comes from the Nahuatl *tlatlaolli*, which means "ground maize." In Puebla and Tlaxcala, they call this "antojito tlatloyo." Tlacoyos are street food, but, at home, they're a favorite snack for la merienda. Tlacoyos are a humble dish with simple preparation. There is another version known as a "huarache" (sandal). It has the same ingredients but is as big as a foot.

3 cups masa harina (white or blue)

1 teaspoon salt

2 cups lukewarm water

1 cup refried beans (canned or homemade)

1 teaspoon cooking oil or lard

1 cup Spicy Tomatillo Salsa with Fresh Chile de Árbol (page 27) or Red Jalapeño Salsa (page 28)

½ cup Mexican crema

1 cup crumbled queso fresco or cotija cheese

1 avocado, pitted and sliced

1. In a medium bowl, whisk together the masa harina and salt. Slowly mix in the water. Work the masa for 15 to 20 minutes, or until it comes away from the bowl, doesn't stick to your fingers, and has a soft, Play-Doh–like texture. Cover it with a damp cloth and set aside.

2. Fill a small bowl with water for wetting your fingers to avoid sticking. Grab a scoop of masa and form a ball the size of your palm or smaller. Repeat to make 8 balls. Keep the balls covered with a damp cloth.

3. Dampen your fingers again. Flatten one ball into a small, thick tortilla. Stuff it with 1 teaspoon of the beans. Close the masa around the beans to form an oval shape and pinch the ends to seal. Repeat with the remaining balls. Keep them covered with a damp cloth.

4. Heat a comal or cast-iron skillet over medium heat. Drop in a few drops of water to check if the comal is hot. When the water sizzles, add the oil. Cook the tlacoyos for 5 to 7 minutes on each side, until toasty brown spots appear.

5. Serve immediately, garnished with the tomatillo salsa, Mexican crema, crumbled queso fresco, and avocado slices.

TIP

Masa harina requires the right amount of water for the right texture: soft but not sticky. You might need more or less than this recipe states, depending on the masa harina brand and its coarseness. Forming tlacoyos takes some practice. Do not fret if the first corn cake is not perfect; the more you practice, the easier it will become.

CEVICHE DE CAMARÓN
SHRIMP CEVICHE

Origin: Sinaloa and Nayarit | Prep time: 45 minutes | Serves 6

The beaches of the Mexican Pacific are the inspiration for this recipe. Typically, ceviche is made with raw seafood and cured in citrus juice, but here, we use precooked shrimp. In Nayarit, there is a paradisiacal place called Bucerias Nuevo Vallarta. The locals visit during the weekend and celebrate by having a feast under a palapa, cheering with a cold beer and eating shrimp ceviche tostadas.

½ cup lime juice

2 tablespoons white vinegar

½ teaspoon garlic puree

¼ teaspoon ground cumin

1 teaspoon sea salt

¼ teaspoon coarse ground black pepper

¼ cup extra-virgin olive oil

1 serrano or jalapeño pepper, finely chopped

1 red onion, finely chopped

2 cups cubed Roma tomatoes

1 pound precooked shrimp, peeled and deveined

½ cup roughly chopped cilantro

Corn chips or tostadas, for serving

1. In a large bowl, whisk together the lime juice, vinegar, and garlic. Add the cumin, salt, and black pepper and whisk again. Add the olive oil slowly, whisking to emulsify. Stir in the serrano, onion, and tomatoes.

2. Incorporate the shrimp and refrigerate, covered, for 15 minutes. When ready to serve, add the cilantro and pair with corn chips or tostadas.

TIP

If you're using precooked frozen shrimp, thaw the shrimp under cold running water or in the refrigerator. If you can find fresh jumbo shrimp, use those instead. Cook the fresh jumbo shrimp in boiling water over high heat for less than 5 minutes, then transfer the shrimp to an ice bath for 10 to 15 minutes. Peel, devein, and remove the tails before preparing the ceviche. Keep the ceviche refrigerated until ready to serve. Eat it the same day.

TORTAS AHOGADAS
DROWNED SANDWICHES

Origin: Jalisco | Prep time: 45 minutes | Cook time: 15 minutes | Serves 4

Drowned tortas are sandwiches drenched in two types of sauce. This dish is a Jalisco staple. Many home cooks pride themselves in making the best tortas ahogadas with salted birote bread, a type of bolillo baguette produced only in the Jalisco region. The sauces, pickled onions, and carnitas can be cooked a day in advance to save time.

For the tomato sauce

4 cups tomato puree

½ white onion

3 cloves

2 garlic cloves

1 bay leaf

1 teaspoon ground cumin

1 teaspoon Mexican oregano

1 tablespoon chicken bouillon

Salt

Freshly ground black pepper

1 teaspoon cooking oil

For the tortas

4 bolillos or small crusty baguettes, halved

1 cup warm Mayocoba Refried Beans (page 111)

4 cups warm shredded carnitas or sliced grilled pork loin

½ cup Chile de Árbol Hot Sauce (page 29)

2 cups Pickled Red Onions (page 33)

To make the tomato sauce

1. In a blender, combine the tomato puree, onion, cloves, garlic, bay leaf, cumin, oregano, bouillon, salt, and pepper and blend for 5 to 7 minutes.

2. In a saucepan over medium heat, warm the oil. Add the sauce and cook for 15 minutes. Cover to keep the sauce warm and set aside.

To assemble the tortas

3. Spread the bolillos with refried beans. Add the carnitas. Close the tortas and place them in single-serving bowls. Ladle some tomato sauce on top and drizzle with hot sauce. Garnish with the pickled onions. Enjoy immediately.

MOLOTES DE QUESO
CHEESE MOLOTES

Origin: Puebla | Prep time: 1 hour | Cook time: 30 minutes | Serves 6

Molotes are a type of crispy thin quesadilla filled with various ingredients: leftovers, cheese, mushrooms, huitlacoche, zucchini flowers, potato, even hot dogs. Molotes is a humble dish celebrated with a fall event every year in San Andres Cholula, where molotes originated. Home cooks in the area pride themselves in making this dish by hand.

4 cups masa harina

1 cup all-purpose flour

1 teaspoon baking soda

½ teaspoon salt

2 cups water, at room temperature, plus more as needed

4 cups frying oil (vegetable or corn, not peanut), plus ½ cup

2 cups shredded Oaxaca or mozzarella cheese

Spicy Tomatillo Salsa with Fresh Chile de Árbol (page 27), for garnish

Mexican crema, for garnish

Shredded lettuce, for garnish

Radishes, for garnish

1. In a large bowl, combine the masa harina with the all-purpose flour, baking soda, and salt. Form a small hole in the middle and add the water, a little bit at a time. (Do not add all the water at once, as it might need more or less.)

2. Work the masa with your hands (or in a stand mixer with a hook) and integrate the remaining water as needed. Continue working the masa for up to 20 minutes (10 minutes if using a mixer), until it doesn't stick to the bowl or your fingers.

3. Transfer the dough to a clean work surface and knead by hand for another 5 minutes. Form the dough into a ball, place it in a medium bowl, and cover it with a damp cloth. Set aside to rest for 30 minutes.

4. While the dough rests, make the plastic squares for pressing the dough. Using scissors, cut off the sealing portion of a gallon freezer bag (the plastic is thicker), and cut down both sides to open the bag completely into two plastic squares.

5. In a deep skillet over medium heat, add 4 cups of oil and bring it to 375°F. Pour the remaining ½ cup of oil into a small bowl.

6. Once the dough has rested, take a portion the size of your palm. Dip the dough in the cold oil and make a dough ball (the oil will help the dough release from the plastic). Put the dough ball on one side of the plastic. Fold the bag over to cover it. Roll the dough ball into a large thin circle. Lift the plastic off one side.

7. Place 1 to 2 tablespoons cheese in the middle of the molote, leaving a distinct border. Fold the plastic over and press the molote edges, removing any air and sealing it until it looks like a large, elongated quesadilla.

8. When the hot oil is ready, gently remove the molote from the plastic and fry it in the oil for 5 minutes on each side, or until golden brown on both sides. Transfer the fried molote to a paper towel–lined plate. Repeat with the remaining dough.

9. Serve the molotes hot, garnished with the salsa verde, Mexican crema, and perhaps shredded lettuce and radishes.

TIP

Molotes dough has to be soft and malleable. Resting it and using the right amount of liquid is key for the best results. The dough has to be rolled thin. Do not stuff the molotes with too much cheese or they won't seal properly, and make sure the frying oil's temperature does not get too hot.

SOPES DE POLLO
CHICKEN MASA HARINA CAKES

Origin: Mexico | Prep time: 30 minutes | Cook time: 20 minutes | Serves 4
Special equipment: comal or cast-iron skillet

Sopes are small masa harina cakes formed in a way that allows for adding many different ingredients. Sopes are a quintessential antojito that dates back to pre-Hispanic times. Some say they originated in Central and South Mexico, but over time, sopes became popular across the country. Depending on the state, sopes are also called "picadas" or "pellizcadas."

2 cups masa harina

½ teaspoon salt

1 cup lukewarm water (more or less, depending on the masa harina)

3 tablespoons cooking oil or lard, plus a few drops

1 cup warm Mayocoba Refried Beans (page 111), or canned

1 cup shredded chicken

3 cups shredded romaine lettuce

1 cup Spicy Tomatillo Salsa with Fresh Chile de Árbol (page 27) or Red Jalapeño Salsa (page 28)

1 cup Mexican crema

½ cup crumbled cotija cheese

1. In a medium bowl, whisk together the masa harina and salt. Slowly mix in the water. Work the masa for 15 to 20 minutes, or until it comes away from the bowl, doesn't stick to your fingers, and has a soft, Play-Doh–like texture. Cover it with a damp cloth and set aside.

2. Fill a small bowl with water for wetting your fingers to avoid sticking. Grab a scoop of masa and form a ball the size of your palm or smaller. Repeat to make 4 to 6 balls. Keep the balls covered with a damp cloth.

3. Use your hands, a tortilla press, or a wood cutting board to flatten the balls, one at a time, into small, thick tortillas.

4. Heat a comal or cast-iron skillet over medium heat. Drop in a few drops of water. When the water sizzles, add a few drops of oil. Cook the tortillas for 5 to 7 minutes on each side, until toasty brown spots appear. Dampen your fingers again and pinch the sides and middle of each corn cake to form sopes.

5. In a skillet, warm the remaining oil. Fry the sopes for a maximum of 3 minutes on each side. Remove excess fat with a napkin. Serve each sope topped with 1 teaspoon of refried beans, shredded chicken, romaine lettuce, tomatillo salsa, Mexican crema, and cotija cheese.

TIP

You can find sopes at many Latino stores. Typical sopes are filled with potatoes and chorizo, or the classic sope is served with shredded chicken and salsa verde.

ANTOJITOS IN MEXICO

The word *antojito* means "small indulgence"—a small bite to tame hunger. Esquites, sopes, quesadillas, chalupas, gorditas, pambazos, tlacoyos, atole, and tamales are all antojitos. In pre-Hispanic times, corn was the primary source of food. In his letters, Fray Bernardino de Sahagún describes antojitos or gorditas as thick tortillas. Tlacoyos were sold in the Tlatelolco Tianguis, a farmers' market during the Aztec Empire.

In the 20th century, antojitos became a substitute for meals due to the hectic lifestyle in large Mexican cities. People working outside of the home needed nourishment. Antojitos became street food. Women set up rudimentary kitchens outside their homes and sold quesadillas and sopes, or they would prepare tamales at home to sell early on the street corner, along with warm atole. Nowadays, everyone eats antojitos.

GORDITAS DE ATOTONILCO CON CHICHARRÓN

ATOTONILCO CORN GORDITAS WITH PORK CRACKLINGS

Origin: Guanajuato | Prep time: 1 hour | Cook time: 40 minutes | Serves 8
Special equipment: tortilla press (optional)

Gorditas are very similar to sopes; however, these are deep-fried. Depending on the region, the fried gorditas could be called *infladitas*, which means "fluffed." These are a fun, easy appetizer or snack.

2 cups masa harina

½ teaspoon salt

2 teaspoons baking powder

1 cup lukewarm water (more or less, depending on the masa harina)

½ cup crushed pork cracklings

¼ cup frying oil

1 cup Grilled Guacamole (page 31)

1 cup Mexican crema

1 cup crumbled queso fresco

1. In a medium bowl, whisk together the masa harina, salt, and baking powder. Slowly mix in the water. Work the masa for 15 to 20 minutes, or until it comes away from the bowl, doesn't stick to your fingers, and has a soft texture. Add the pork cracklings and mix well. Form the dough into balls the size of your palm and set aside.

2. Using scissors, cut off the sealing portion of a gallon freezer bag (the plastic is thicker), and cut down both sides to open the bag completely into two plastic squares. Open the tortilla press (if using) and lay out one of the plastic squares. Place one dough ball on top of the plastic and cover it with the second plastic square. Clamp down the tortilla press and press gently. (Or use your hands to form a round gordita.) The gordita should be thick, not thin. Remove the gordita from the press and carefully peel off the plastic. Repeat with the rest of the dough balls.

3. Heat the oil in a deep fryer between 350°F and 375°F. Test the oil by frying a small portion of dough. If it fries fast, it is too hot.

4. Fry the gorditas for about 5 minutes on each side, until golden brown and puffed. Transfer to a paper towel–covered plate to absorb excess oil.

5. Serve topped with guacamole, Mexican crema, and queso fresco.

TIP

Try to find thick pork cracklings with pieces of meat. Process the cracklings in a food processor, or put the cracklings in a plastic bag and crush them with a mallet.

FLAUTAS DE CARNE DESHEBRADA

CRISPY BEEF TACOS

Origin: Sinaloa and Mexico | Prep time: 30 minutes | Cook time: 30 minutes | Serves 4

Flautas are long, thin, rolled crispy tacos that resemble a flute. The dish was created in Sinaloa to repurpose meat leftovers. However, it is consumed in many states, including Mexico City, where flautas are a favorite in many households because they are both delicious and economical.

12 large corn or flour tortillas

3 cups shredded beef or chicken

1 cup frying oil

3 cups shredded romaine lettuce

1 cup guacamole

1 cup Spicy Tomatillo Salsa with Fresh Chile de Árbol (page 27)

1 cup shredded queso fresco

1 cup Mexican crema

1. Warm the tortillas first for easy rolling. Add a small amount of beef to the center of each tortilla and roll tightly. Set aside.

2. Heat the oil in a deep skillet to 375°F. Fry the flautas, a few at a time, until golden brown (about 2 to 3 minutes), and then transfer them with tongs to a paper towel–covered plate to absorb excess oil.

3. Serve garnished with lettuce, guacamole, tomatillo salsa, queso fresco, and Mexican crema.

VARIATION

You can stuff flautas with other ingredients, such as potato, cheese, or carnitas. The flautas can be prepared a day in advance, but fry them just before eating.

MEMELAS OAXAQUEÑAS
OAXACAN MEMELAS

Origin: Oaxaca | Prep time: 45 minutes, plus 20 minutes to rest
Cook time: 30 minutes | Serves 6 | Special equipment: tortilla press, comal

The name "memela" comes from the Nahuatl *mimilli*, which means tortilla. Memelas are common in Chiapas, Tlaxcala, Puebla, and Veracruz. Large versions are known as huaraches ("sandals"). Another name is tetelas. In Oaxaca, memelas are small and round and typically made with blue corn and pork lard.

2 cups masa harina (white or blue)

1 teaspoon salt

2 cups lukewarm water (or less)

1 tablespoon pork lard, at room temperature, plus ¼ cup melted

1 cup Mayocoba Refried Beans (page 111), or canned

1 cup crumbled cotija cheese

1 cup finely chopped white onion

1 cup Spicy Tomatillo Salsa with Fresh Chile de Árbol (page 27) or Red Jalapeño Salsa (page 28)

½ cup cilantro leaves

1. In a medium bowl, whisk together the masa harina and salt. Slowly mix in the water until uniform. Add the room-temperature lard and continue working the masa until it comes away from the bowl, doesn't stick to your fingers, and has a soft texture. Allow the masa to rest for at least 20 minutes covered with plastic.

2. While the dough rests, make the plastic squares for the tortilla press. Using scissors, cut off the sealing portion of a gallon freezer bag (the plastic is thicker), and cut down both sides to open the bag completely into two plastic squares.

3. Open the tortilla press and lay one plastic square on the press. Grab a small portion of the dough and form a ball. Place the ball on the press and cover it with the second plastic square. Clamp down the tortilla press and press gently once to create a round, thick tortilla.

4. Remove the tortilla from the press and carefully peel off the plastic.

5. In a comal, cook each memela for 5 to 7 minutes on each side, until browning spots appear. Remove the memela from the pan, wet your fingers in cold water, and pinch the sides and the middle while still warm.

6. Add a few drops of the melted lard to the bottom of the memela and top it with refried beans and cheese. Return it to the comal and cook for another 5 minutes.

7. Serve hot, garnished with onions, salsa, and cilantro.

TIP
Pork lard makes the memelas authentic, but if you cannot find it or don't want to use it, use butter instead.

SOUPS AND STEWS

POZOLE
POZOLE

Origin: Mexico and Guerrero | Prep time: 15 minutes | Cook time: 40 minutes
Serves 6 | Special equipment: Instant Pot or pressure cooker, blender

"Pozole" comes from the Nahuatl *pozolli*, which means "frothy" and references the foam the boiling corn creates. The Aztecs considered pozole a sacred dish and made it for religious ceremonies. After the Spanish conquest, pozole became a dish served at weddings, festivals, and special celebrations. Each region has its spin and flavor profiles on one of the most ancient and traditional Mexican dishes.

For the pozole

1 pound pork loin, cut into large chunks

1 tablespoon dried oregano

1 teaspoon ground cumin

2 tablespoons chicken bouillon

1 teaspoon corn oil

4 cups chicken broth

2 cups water

4 cups cooked canned hominy

3 bay leaves

1 cup sliced red radishes

1 cup chopped red onion

4 cups shredded iceberg lettuce

2 limes, quartered

For the red sauce

4 guajillo chiles, seeded and stemmed

1 cup hot water

2 garlic cloves, roasted

1 tablespoon chicken bouillon

1 teaspoon ground cumin

1 teaspoon Mexican oregano

1 teaspoon cooking oil

Salt (optional)

To make the pozole

1. Season the pork with the oregano, cumin, and bouillon.

2. In a skillet, heat the oil and sear the pork until golden brown.

3. Transfer the pork to an Instant Pot or pressure cooker. Add the broth, water, hominy, and bay leaves. Seal the cooker and choose "Meat/Stew" mode. Cook for 40 minutes. Allow the pressure to release naturally.

4. Serve the pozole hot, garnished with the radishes, onion, and lettuce. Enjoy it white with a few drops of lime juice, or add red sauce to make it a red pozole.

To make the red sauce

5. Soak the chiles in the hot water for 10 to 15 minutes, until soft. Reserve ½ cup of the chile soaking water.

6. Transfer the peppers and reserved soaking water to a blender. Add the garlic, bouillon, cumin, and oregano and blend.

7. Strain the sauce into the saucepan, add the oil, and cook for 10 to 15 minutes. Taste and add salt (if using).

8. Serve the red sauce in a medium bowl and use it to garnish the pozole.

TIP
Cut the pork loin into big chunks, as it tends to shrink while cooking in the pressure cooker. Searing the pork loin first adds flavor and allows even browning. This recipe also works with chicken or turkey. The pozole and sauce keep well in airtight containers in the refrigerator for several days.

FOOD AND TRADITIONS FOR MEXICO'S DAY OF THE DEAD

November 2 is the day families all over Mexico remember and celebrate those who have passed. Traditions include visiting tombs and putting up an altar with candles, paper decorations, symbols, photos of the beloved departed, and food and beverages that the departed enjoyed when alive to help them in their journey to return home. Mexican families spread cempasúchil flower petals at the home's entrance to allow the souls to find their way home to enjoy the feast. Typical dishes are pan de muerto, café de olla, chicken with mole, carnitas, and pozole, all served with homemade corn tortillas, horchata, or hibiscus flower agua fresca. Candy skulls, candied pumpkin, and camote are on the menu. Depending on the state, the pan de muerto that is baked only for this day can change. In Oaxaca, it is called pan de yema and has anise notes, whereas in Mexico City, the bread has hints of orange blossom water.

SOPA DE TORTILLA
TORTILLA SOUP

Origin: Tlaxcala and Mexico | Prep time: 30 minutes | Cook time: 1 hour | Serves 6

This soup, also called sopa Azteca, originated in Tlaxcala, the land of maize, before becoming one of the most famous soups all over Mexico. The classic recipe is a luscious soup with a characteristic toasty flavor that pairs well with avocado chunks, chicharróns, queso fresco, and Mexican crema. My mom used to make this soup for my birthday. It's a feast.

1 ancho chile, seeded and stemmed

1 pasilla chile, seeded and stemmed

1 cup hot water

1 teaspoon cooking oil

½ medium white onion, diced

2 garlic cloves

8 to 10 Roma tomatoes, halved

1 tablespoon chicken bouillon

12 corn tortillas, cut into strips and fried

4 cups chicken stock

4 fresh epazote leaves or 1 teaspoon dried

Salt (optional)

1 avocado, diced

1 cup diced queso fresco

1 cup pork rinds (optional)

½ cup Mexican crema

1. Soak the ancho and pasilla chiles in the water for 15 minutes, or until soft. Reserve ½ cup of the chile soaking water.

2. In a skillet, heat the oil. Sauté the onion for 5 minutes. Add the garlic and sauté for 3 minutes. Add the tomatoes and bouillon and cook for 8 minutes.

3. Transfer the peppers and reserved soaking water to a blender. Add the vegetable mixture and a handful of fried tortilla strips. Blend.

4. Transfer the mixture to a saucepan over medium heat and cook for 10 to 15 minutes. When the sauce starts bubbling, add the stock and epazote. Simmer for 30 minutes. Taste and add salt (if using).

5. Serve with a handful of fried tortilla strips. Garnish with avocado, queso fresco, pork rinds (if using), and ribbons of Mexican crema.

SOPA TARASCA
TARASCA SOUP

Origin: Michoacán | Prep time: 30 minutes | Cook time: 35 minutes
Serves 6 | Special equipment: blender

This dish honors the Purépecha heritage and the Tarasco civilization of Michoacán. The soup is similar to tortilla soup but has pinto beans mixed into the broth. This is a humble but flavorful dish, and it is a staple of this region.

1 tablespoon cooking oil

1 ancho chile, seeded and stemmed, plus 1 chile seeded, stemmed, sliced, and fried, for garnish

½ roasted small white onion

2 garlic cloves, roasted

4 Roma tomatoes, roasted, peeled, and seeded

2 tablespoons chicken bouillon

3 cups water or vegetable stock, divided, plus a little for blending

2½ cups canned pinto beans

Salt (optional)

2 cups fried tortilla strips, for garnish

½ avocado diced, for garnish

½ cup Mexican crema, for garnish

½ cup cotija cheese, for garnish

1. Heat the oil in a soup pot over medium heat and quick-fry the ancho chile for 2 to 3 minutes. Set aside. In the same oil, fry the onion, garlic, and tomatoes.

2. Season the fried vegetables with the bouillon and add 1 cup of water and the fried ancho chile. Simmer for 7 to 10 minutes, until the chile is soft.

3. Transfer the mixture to a blender with the beans and a little water. Blend on high. Pour the blended soup into the soup pot and add the remaining 2 cups of water. Simmer for 15 to 20 minutes. Taste and add salt (if using).

4. Serve hot, garnished with tortilla strips, fried ancho, avocado, Mexican crema, and cheese.

TIP
Replace the vegetable stock with homemade bean broth for a more authentic result. To make this dish vegetarian, replace the chicken bouillon with vegetable bouillon. The roasting provides a smoky note, but it can be skipped; just sauté the onion, garlic, and tomatoes with the oil.

BIRRIA CLÁSICA
CLASSIC BIRRIA

Origin: Jalisco | Prep time: 15 minutes | Cook time: 1 hour 10 minutes | Serves 8
Special equipment: Instant Pot or pressure cooker, blender

This 17th-century recipe originated in Atequiza, Jalisco, which is known as the world's birria capital. Birria is a spicy, fatty lamb consommé. Nowadays, birria is a popular dish among families from all over Mexico who prepare it for Sunday brunch. Typical birria uses lamb; however, in certain areas, it is made with goat or beef. Do not confuse birria with barbacoa, which is a barbecued lamb broth prepared using a different technique and is not spicy.

1 pound lamb spareribs or loin chops, cut into chunks

1 pound boneless lamb shoulder, cut into large chunks

1 tablespoon ground cumin

1 teaspoon coarse sea salt

1 tablespoon freshly ground black pepper

1 tablespoon cooking oil

2 ancho chiles, stemmed and seeded

3 guajillo chiles, stemmed and seeded

2 chiles de árbol, stemmed and seeded (optional)

1 small onion, cut into chunks

3 garlic cloves

3 large Roma tomatoes, halved

4 whole allspice berries

3 cloves

1 cinnamon stick or 1 teaspoon ground

1 teaspoon Mexican oregano

1 teaspoon marjoram

2 bay leaves

1 tablespoon beef bouillon

2 cups beef stock

¼ cup apple cider vinegar

3 carrots, peeled and cut into thick sticks

4 cups water

Salt (optional)

1. Season the lamb spareribs and shoulder with the cumin, salt, and pepper.

2. Set the Instant Pot or pressure cooker to the "Sauté" mode. Add the oil and quick-fry the ancho, guajillo, and árbol chiles for 3 minutes or less. Remove and set aside.

3. Sauté the onion and garlic. Add the tomatoes, allspice, cloves, cinnamon, oregano, marjoram, bay leaves, and bouillon. Cook for 7 minutes. Add the fried chiles and stock and simmer for another 15 minutes, or until the chiles are soft. Remove and reserve the bay leaves, allspice, and cinnamon stick.

4. Transfer the mixture to a blender and blend into a sauce. Strain and return it to the pot. Return the bay leaves, cinnamon, and allspice to the pot as well. Add the lamb, vinegar, carrots, and water. Taste and add salt (if using). Seal the lid and cook on high for 30 to 45 minutes. If using a regular pressure cooker, cook for 1 hour. Allow the pressure to release naturally. Prepare and serve as desired.

TIP

Shred the birria for tacos. Have some shredded Jack cheese handy. Submerge tortillas in the birria broth and stuff them with cheese and shredded meat. Or fold, fry, and serve the tacos paired with a cup of birria consommé, garnished with chopped onion, fresh cilantro, lime juice, and drops of Dried Chile Oil Sauce (page 32).

VARIATION

Replace the lamb with beef chamberete, beef cheeks, lean beef, or oxtail. This consommé must be fatty, so the beef requires a mix of lean and fatty cuts. This dish is best when cooked the night before to allow the flavors to develop.

SOPA DE LIMA
LIME SOUP

Origin: Yucatán | Prep time: 30 minutes | Cook time: 1 hour | Serves 6
Special equipment: cast-iron Dutch oven

Sopa de lima is an aromatic, flavorful comfort food from Yucatán. Originally, the soup was created by Maya cooks using wild turkey. With the Spanish conquest and the arrival of citrus and chickens, the soup transformed into what we know today. This version uses chicken and the same condiments the Mayas used.

1½ tablespoons cooking oil, divided

2 bay leaves

2 cloves

2 whole allspice berries

1 teaspoon Mexican oregano

½ cinnamon stick

2 large skinless, bone-in chicken breasts

3 garlic cloves, charred

6 cups water or chicken stock

1 tablespoon chicken bouillon or salt

½ red onion, chopped

2 large ají dulce (sweet peppers), chopped, or 1 green bell pepper

2 cups diced and seeded Roma tomatoes

2 limas, sliced (or yellow lemons)

¼ cup lime juice

2 to 3 cups fried tortilla strips, for serving

½ cup Habanero-Tomato Salsa (page 30), for serving

1. Heat 1 tablespoon of oil in a cast-iron Dutch oven over medium heat. Add the bay leaves, cloves, allspice, oregano, and cinnamon and sauté for 3 minutes or less.

2. Add the chicken and garlic. Pour the water over the top and add the bouillon. Cover and simmer for 30 to 45 minutes. When the chicken is ready, remove it from the Dutch oven and shred it. Strain the chicken broth and set it aside.

3. Heat the remaining ½ tablespoon of oil in the same pot over medium heat. Add the onion and cook for 3 minutes. Add the ají dulce and cook for another 5 minutes. Then, add the tomatoes and cook until soft.

4. Combine the mixture with the strained broth. Incorporate the chicken, limas, and lime juice. Cover and simmer the soup over low heat for 7 to 10 minutes. Take care not to boil the soup.

5. Serve with fried tortilla strips and topped with salsa.

CALDILLO DE RES CON PAPAS
BEEF AND POTATO STEW

Origin: Chihuahua and Durango | Prep time: 30 minutes | Cook time: 45 minutes
Serves 6 | Special equipment: cast-iron Dutch oven

Caldillo is a comforting, homey, brothy stew perfect for a winter day and when we need to feel closer to home. This version is my great-grandmother's recipe. My great-grandfather loved adding chopped serrano pepper to this soup and garnishing it with cilantro. This caldillo is common in Durango, too. It became famous as the dish used to feed the workers responsible for building the railroad in the 1900s.

1 pound beef filet, cut into chunks

1 teaspoon salt

½ teaspoon freshly ground black pepper

1½ tablespoons cooking oil, divided

½ white onion, diced

2 garlic cloves, chopped

2 Roma tomatoes, seeded and diced

1 tablespoon beef bouillon

2 large or 3 small yellow potatoes, peeled and cut into chunks

2 cups beef stock

3 cups water

2 poblano peppers, roasted, seeded, peeled, and cut into strips

Chihuahua-Style Flour Tortillas (page 24), for serving

1. Season the beef with the salt and black pepper. Set aside.

2. Preheat a cast-iron Dutch oven over high heat. Pour 1 tablespoon of oil into the Dutch oven and reduce the heat to medium. Add the beef and sear for 5 to 7 minutes. Remove the beef from the Dutch oven and set aside.

3. Add the remaining ½ tablespoon of oil to the Dutch oven and sauté the onion for 5 minutes. Add the garlic, tomatoes, and bouillon and cook for 5 minutes, stirring to avoid sticking.

4. Add the potatoes, beef, stock, and water and simmer for 10 minutes. Add the peppers and stir again. Cook, covered, for another 15 to 20 minutes, until the potatoes are tender.

5. Serve the caldillo hot with flour tortillas.

CALDO DE CAMARÓN O HUATAPÉ

HUATAPÉ SHRIMP BROTH

Origin: Tamaulipas | Prep time: 30 minutes | Cook time: 45 minutes | Serves 6
Special equipment: blender

Huatapé's roots are Nahua and Totonac, and the meaning of *huatapé* is "to eat chile." In the north of Veracruz, they make it green using jalapeños and epazote. Others make it with pork, chicken, and potatoes.

½ white onion

3 garlic cloves

4 large Roma tomatoes, halved and seeded

3 ancho chiles, stemmed, seeded, and soaked in hot water, with ½ cup soaking water reserved

1 tablespoon cooking oil

2 tablespoons shrimp bouillon

Salt

Freshly ground black pepper

4 cups water, or 2 cans shrimp broth and 2 cups water

2 tablespoons masa harina, diluted with ½ cup water

5 epazote leaves

1 pound fresh large shrimp, peeled and deveined

Lime wedges, for serving

Dried Chile Oil Sauce (page 32), for serving

1. In a blender, combine the onion, garlic, tomatoes, and chiles with the reserved chile soaking water. Blend on high to a thick sauce.

2. Heat the oil in a soup pot over medium heat. Add the blended mixture and cook for 15 minutes.

3. Season the soup with the bouillon, salt, and black pepper. Simmer for 5 minutes, then add the water. Cover the pot and cook for 15 minutes more.

4. Add the masa harina and whisk until thick. Add the epazote. Cook for another 5 minutes.

5. Five minutes before serving, add the shrimp to the soup and cook for 3 to 4 minutes, until pink. Serve the soup hot with lime wedges and dried chile oil sauce.

SOPA SECA DE FIDEO
MEXICAN FIDEO SOUP

Origin: Mexico City | Prep time: 30 minutes | Cook time: 30 minutes | Serves 6

Fideo is a quintessential homestyle dish, originating in the 17th century. It is rooted in the Spanish heritage. The secret to a delicious fideo is frying the pasta and using chipotle in adobo sauce.

½ cup cooking oil

7 ounces fideo pasta

1 cup Mexican-style canned tomato puree with jalapeño

½ chipotle en adobo, or ½ teaspoon chipotle sauce (see steps 1 and 3 of Chicken in Creamy Chipotle Sauce, page 80)

1 tablespoon chicken bouillon or salt

½ teaspoon freshly ground black pepper

1 cup water

½ cup crumbled queso fresco

½ cup Mexican crema

1 avocado, sliced

1. Heat the oil to 250°F in a large saucepan over medium heat. Add the fideo pasta and fry for about 2 minutes, until golden brown. Transfer the pasta to a paper towel–lined plate and set aside. Remove and discard any excess oil from the pan.

2. In the same saucepan over low heat, combine the tomato puree, chipotle en adobo, bouillon, and black pepper. Simmer the sauce for 7 to 10 minutes.

3. Add the water and fideo. Stir and cook, covered, for 10 to 15 minutes, until the liquid has been absorbed and the pasta is tender.

4. Serve garnished with the queso fresco, ribbons of Mexican crema, and avocado.

TIP

You can use the same method to prepare any short pasta, such as shells, stars, and letters. Use queso Oaxaca or queso Chihuahua. Avoid adding more liquid than necessary. Omit the chicken bouillon and use salt for a vegetarian version.

98 TAMALES DE CERDO

MAIN COURSES

PESCADO A LA VERACRUZANA
VERACRUZ FISH

Origin: Veracruz | Prep time: 30 minutes | Cook time: 35 minutes | Serves 4

This dish from Sotavento, Veracruz, is prepared with huachinango (red snapper), a fish common in the area. Typically, the fish is cooked whole and poached in tomato sauce. This recipe is a clear example of how two culinary cultures incorporate ingredients from the old world, local favorites, and hot peppers. Pescado a la Veracruzana is a family favorite for Lent, too.

4 fillets red snapper or rockfish

½ teaspoon coarse salt

1 tablespoon olive oil

½ white onion, sliced

3 garlic cloves, minced

4 cups diced tomatoes

2 bay leaves

1 teaspoon dried oregano or marjoram

1 tablespoon chicken bouillon

2 cups tomato puree

4 tablespoons pimento-stuffed Spanish olives

2 tablespoons capers

½ cup fish broth or water

4 whole pickled jalapeños

1 pound boiler potatoes, peeled and cooked

Cooked white rice, for serving

1. Season the snapper with the salt and refrigerate, covered, for 30 minutes.

2. Heat the oil in a sauté pan over medium heat. Add the onion and sauté for 5 minutes. Stir in the garlic, tomatoes, bay leaves, oregano, and bouillon.

3. Add the tomato puree and cook for another 7 minutes. Stir in the olives and capers.

4. Add the broth and simmer for 10 minutes. Add the jalapeños, lower the heat, and continue cooking, covered, for 5 minutes.

5. Incorporate the potatoes and snapper and cook, covered, for another 5 to 7 minutes. Serve the fish with the sauce and a side of white rice.

CAMARONES ENDIABLADOS
SHRIMP DIABLO

Origin: Guerrero | Prep time: 15 minutes | Cook time: 25 minutes | Serves 4

Shrimp diablo is a classic in Mexican cuisine, typically served at parties and special occasions because shrimp are a luxury ingredient. This dish is typical during Lent, too. After cooking it only once, everyone in your family will want this dish on the weekly menu. It is one of those dinner dishes that looks fancy but is easy to prepare.

1 pound fresh large shrimp, cleaned and deveined

1 teaspoon sazón Latino (see tip)

1½ tablespoons olive oil, divided

1 garlic clove, chopped

4 cups tomato puree

2 tablespoons chipotle sauce (see steps 1 and 3 of Chicken in Creamy Chipotle Sauce, page 80)

1 thyme sprig

2 bay leaves

1 tablespoon (or 1 cube) shrimp bouillon

4 cups cooked white rice

1. In a medium bowl, combine the shrimp and sazón Latino. Set aside.

2. Heat 1 tablespoon of oil in a skillet over medium heat. Add the shrimp and sauté for about 2 minutes, until they turn opaque. Set aside.

3. Heat the remaining ½ tablespoon of oil in a saucepan over medium heat. Add the garlic and sauté for 2 minutes or less. Stir in the tomato puree, chipotle sauce, thyme, bay leaves, and bouillon. Cover and cook for 10 to 15 minutes.

4. Reduce the heat to low, stir in the shrimp, and simmer for 2 minutes. Serve over a bed of white rice.

TIP

Sazón Latino is a seasoning mix that can be found in the international foods aisle at many grocery stores. Or make your own by mixing equal amounts of oregano, cumin, and freshly ground black pepper. Add salt as needed. The shrimp bouillon can be replaced with chicken bouillon.

ARROZ A LA TUMBADA
TUMBADA RICE

Origin: Veracruz | Prep time: 30 minutes | Cook time: 55 minutes | Serves 8
Special equipment: blender

Tumbado or *tumbada* means "to throw." Urban legend says that an inexperienced fisherman created this recipe by throwing all the seafood he had on hand into a pot, resulting in a mix between paella and seafood soup.

½ white onion, roasted

3 garlic cloves, roasted

3 Roma tomatoes, roasted and peeled

1 or 2 jalapeño peppers, roasted

1 tablespoon tomato paste

2½ cups water, divided

2 tablespoons chicken or shrimp bouillon

6 cups seafood broth, divided

Salt

Freshly ground black pepper

4 tablespoons olive oil

2 cups long-grain rice, presoaked and drained

1 bunch epazote or cilantro

4 uncooked crab legs, or 2 cups crabmeat

10 clams, in the shell

1 cup cooked octopus chunks

2 thick, uncooked red snapper fillets, skin-on and cut into large chunks

6 large uncooked, unpeeled, deveined shrimp

1. In a blender, combine the onion, garlic, tomatoes, jalapeño, tomato paste, and ½ cup of water. Blend into a puree.

2. In a deep sauté pan over medium heat, add the puree and cook for 5 minutes. Add the bouillon and 1 cup of seafood broth and cook for another 7 minutes. Season with salt and black pepper. Set aside. This sauce needs to be a bit salty, as it is the base that will flavor all the seafood.

3. Heat the oil in a separate skillet over medium heat. Add the rice and fry for 7 minutes, until toasty and well coated. Add the rice to the tomato puree and stir. Pour in the remaining 5 cups of seafood broth and 2 cups of water.

4. Add the epazote, crabs, and clams. Cover and continue cooking over medium heat for 15 to 20 minutes. Add the octopus and red snapper and cover again.

5. Check the water level. Add more fish stock or water, if needed. This dish is liquidy but not a soup. Taste and add more salt, if needed. Cook for another 10 minutes. Add the shrimp, cover, and cook for 5 to 7 minutes, until pink.

TIP

The octopus can be cooked in a pressure cooker with salt, onion, and bay leaves, or it can be seasoned with your favorite seafood mix and grilled. Some fisheries sell it precooked and ready to use. If you prefer not to add it, substitute another seafood of your choice.

INTRODUCTION OF PORK TO MEXICO

Some of the things the Spanish conquest brought to Mexico were condiments, olive oil, rice, sugar, garlic, and onions. The Spaniards also brought domesticated animals, such as sheep, cows, chickens, goats, and pigs. Hernán Cortés was responsible for introducing pork to la Nueva España. Many of these pigs were Iberian, Celtic, Neapolitan, and Asian. Cross breeding created the Mexican hairless pig, a breed raised for more than a century by the Mayas, who called it *t'ooroch k'eek'een*. Since then, the industry has evolved, and nowadays, most pork consumed in Mexico comes from local farms and American swine have replaced the Mexican hairless pig. However, traditional backyard pig production still exists. If there had been no Spanish conquest, tacos al pastor, cochinita, chicharrón, lard, and the many pork dishes we enjoy today would not have existed. Did you know the Spaniards also brought the frying technique? Slow cooking and frying in pork lard are what makes carnitas so unique.

PESCADO A LA TALLA
GUERRERO-STYLE FISH

Origin: Guerrero | Prep time: 1 hour | Cook time: 1 hour 15 minutes | Serves 4 to 6
Special equipment: charcoal grill, blender, grilling basket

This dish was created half a century ago by Gloria Suazo, a home cook turned restaurant owner in the 1970s. She still owns the humble palapa converted into an eatery in Barra Vieja. I have enjoyed this dish while watching the big waves and the unforgettable Acapulco sunrise.

1 tablespoon cooking oil, plus more for brushing

½ onion, cut into chunks

2 garlic cloves

3 guajillo chiles, seeded and stemmed

2 ancho chiles, seeded and stemmed

1½ cups water

1 teaspoon cumin

1 teaspoon marjoram

1 teaspoon freshly ground black pepper

1 tablespoon chicken bouillon

1 large red snapper, butterflied

½ cup mayonnaise

1 cup adobo sauce, for basting

1 cup melted butter, for basting

1. Preheat a charcoal grill to between 400°F and 450°F.

2. In a skillet, heat the oil over high heat and fry the onion for 5 to 7 minutes, until golden brown. Reduce the heat to medium, add the garlic, and sauté for 5 minutes. Add the guajillo and ancho chiles and fry for 2 minutes, stirring constantly. Add the water and cook for 15 minutes, or until the chiles are soft.

3. Transfer the mixture to a blender and blend until smooth. Strain and return the sauce to the skillet. Season the mixture with the cumin, marjoram, black pepper, and bouillon. Cook for another 10 minutes. Remove the skillet from heat and set aside to cool.

4. Open the grilling basket and brush it with oil. Place the snapper on one side, skin-side down. Brush evenly with the mayonnaise, and then with some adobo sauce.

5. Close the grilling basket and grill for 5 minutes. Turn the fish and grill for another 5 minutes. Turn the fish again. Add more adobo to moisten the fish and grill again. In total, you will turn the fish six to eight times, cooking it for 5 minutes each time, until it shows grilling marks. Between turns, baste the fish with more adobo sauce and the melted butter.

6. Open the grilling basket and serve the fish on a large plate.

JAIBAS RELLENAS
STUFFED CRABS

Origin: Tamaulipas | Prep time: 15 minutes | Cook time: 35 minutes | Serves 4

This is a quintessential dish from Tamaulipas and the symbol of the city of Tampico, but it is also enjoyed in Veracruz. There are many ways to make this dish, but all versions are delicious and simple to prepare. You can use cooked crabmeat and shell-shaped plates for serving, or use the crab stuffing for making empanadas or croquettes.

2 tablespoons olive oil

1 small white onion, finely chopped

2 garlic cloves

1 cup diced Roma tomatoes

2 cups cooked crabmeat

1 tablespoon Chile de Árbol Hot Sauce (page 29)

¼ cup cilantro leaves, chopped

4 crab shells, cleaned

2 tablespoons bread crumbs

1 tablespoon butter

4 cups shredded lettuce

2 limes, quartered

1. Preheat the oven to 375°F.

2. Heat the oil in a sauté pan over medium heat. Add the onion and sauté for 2 to 3 minutes, until translucent. Add the garlic and sauté for another 2 minutes. Stir in the tomatoes and cook for 5 minutes.

3. Reduce the heat to low and add the crabmeat and hot sauce. Mix and simmer, covered, for 15 minutes. Remove the sauté pan from the heat and mix the cilantro into the crab stuffing.

4. Stuff the crab shells with the stuffing and arrange them on a baking sheet. Sprinkle the stuffed shells with the bread crumbs and dot them with the butter. Bake for 10 minutes, or until the bread crumbs are toasted.

5. Serve over a bed of lettuce with a lime wedge.

TIP
Many fish counters sell cooked crabmeat and clean shells. If you cannot find crab shells, use mini pie pans or purchase Nantucket scallop shells on Amazon.

POLLO EN SALSA CREMOSA DE CHIPOTLES
CHICKEN IN CREAMY CHIPOTLE SAUCE

Origin: Mexico | Prep time: 15 minutes | Cook time: 45 minutes | Serves 4
Special equipment: blender

Chicken dishes are lifesavers for many busy moms. I know my mom sometimes was out of ideas and would get inspired watching a cooking TV show segment. She recreated this recipe using the tips of a famous home cook named Chepina Peralta.

1 tablespoon cooking oil

2 garlic cloves

½ white onion, cut into chunks

4 skinless chicken breasts

1 teaspoon salt

Pinch freshly ground black pepper

1 cup Mexican crema or heavy (whipping) cream

1 cup evaporated milk

8 ounces cream cheese

2 canned chipotles in adobo

2 tablespoons chipotle adobo sauce

1 tablespoon chicken bouillon

½ cup fresh milk

Mexican white rice, for serving

Shredded cotija cheese or crumbled queso fresco, for serving

1. In a skillet, heat the oil over medium heat and fry the garlic for 2 minutes. Add the onion and fry for 5 to 7 minutes, until the onion and garlic are golden brown. Remove from heat and set aside.

2. Season the chicken with the salt and pepper and fry it in the skillet over medium heat for 5 to 7 minutes per side, or until it reaches an internal temperature of 165°F. Remove the skillet from the heat, cover with a lid, and set aside.

3. In a blender, combine the onion mixture, cream, milk, cream cheese, chipotles, adobo sauce, and bouillon. Blend for 3 minutes, until smooth.

4. Return the skillet to very low heat. Pour the fresh milk into the skillet, add the chicken, and then the sauce. Mix well, cover, and cook for 10 to 15 minutes. Do not boil as the sauce could curdle.

5. Serve the chicken with creamy chipotle sauce and a side of Mexican white rice. Garnish with shredded cotija cheese or crumbled queso fresco.

POLLO PIBIL
CHICKEN PIBIL

Origin: Yucatán | Prep time: 10 minutes, plus at least 1 hour to marinate
Cook time: 30 minutes | Serves 4 to 6 | Special equipment: food processor,
Instant Pot or pressure cooker

The word "pibil" comes from the ancient Maya technique of cooking meat wrapped in banana leaves in an underground oven made of stone and wood called a pib. This tradition still exists but is used only when catering for parties or special events. The pibil sauce used in chicken or cochinita pibil is called recado, and it is a fusion of many cuisines, including Maya, French, and Caribbean. It is incredible how a condiment can represent cultural heritage in such a delicious way.

1 (3.5-ounce) package achiote or annatto paste

3 cups orange juice

½ cup apple cider vinegar

3 garlic cloves

3 teaspoons Mexican oregano

1 teaspoon ground cumin

2 teaspoons salt

4 bone-in, skin-on chicken breasts

1 tablespoon pork lard or cooking oil

3 bay leaves

1 large banana leaf, fresh or frozen and thawed (optional)

Mexican Rice (page 108), for serving

Warm corn tortillas, for serving

1 cup Pickled Red Onions (page 33), for serving

1. In a food processor, combine the achiote paste, orange juice, vinegar, garlic, oregano, cumin, and salt. Process for 5 to 7 minutes into a sauce.

2. Put the chicken and sauce in a covered container. Refrigerate for at least 1 hour or up to overnight. The longer the chicken marinates, the better flavor it will have. Remove from the marinade.

3. Set an Instant Pot to the "Sauté" function. Heat the lard. Remove the chicken from the marinade and sear it on both sides in the pot. Add the bay leaves and all the marinade to the pot. Cover the chicken with the banana leaf (if using); this will provide an authentic flavor.

4. Seal the pressure cooker and set to high. Cook for 30 minutes, then perform a quick release. Remove the bones from the chicken and serve with a side of Mexican rice, warm corn tortillas, and pickled onions.

MOLE POBLANO CON POLLO
CHICKEN IN POBLANO MOLE

Origin: Puebla | Prep time: 1 hour | Cook time: 1 hour 50 minutes | Serves 8
Special equipment: blender

Mole originated many years ago in Puebla, where nuns from the Convent of Santa Rosa developed this recipe. The original recipe calls for many ingredients that provide the unique flavor of this magical sauce. In my search for simplified recipes for effortless cooking, I developed this mole that is as tasty as the original but can be prepared at home easily.

For the chicken

1 whole chicken, cut into segments

½ white onion

2 garlic cloves

2 carrots, peeled and halved

3 celery sticks, including leaves

1 bunch fresh cilantro

6 cups water

1 tablespoon chicken bouillon

For the mole sauce

4 ancho chiles, stemmed and seeded

4 mulato chiles, stemmed and seeded

5 guajillo chiles, stemmed and seeded

3 cups hot water

1 cup roasted peanuts

2 medium tomatoes, roasted

3 garlic cloves, roasted

½ white onion, roasted

⅓ cup peanut butter or almond butter

½ overripe plantain, cut into rounds

2 to 3 cups chicken broth

90 grams (about 3 ounces) Mexican chocolate, broken into pieces

1 teaspoon ground cumin

1 teaspoon ground cinnamon

½ teaspoon ground cloves

1 tablespoon chicken bouillon

Salt

3 tablespoons sesame seeds, toasted

Mexican Rice (page 108), for serving

Frijoles de olla, for serving

Warm corn tortillas, for serving

To make the chicken

1. In a deep soup pot with a lid, combine the chicken, onion, garlic, carrots, celery, cilantro, water, and bouillon. Cover and cook over low heat for 45 minutes. Do not allow the water to boil if you prefer a clear broth. (Or cook in an Instant Pot on high for 20 to 30 minutes, with a quick pressure release.) Remove the chicken. Strain the broth into a sealable container and freeze or refrigerate for later use.

To make the mole sauce

2. Soak the ancho, mulato, and guajillo peppers in the hot water for 10 to 15 minutes until soft. Reserve 1½ cups of the chile soaking water.

3. Meanwhile, in a skillet over medium heat, toast the peanuts for 5 to 7 minutes, constantly stirring to avoid burning. Set aside.

4. In a blender, combine the soaked chiles, reserved soaking water, tomatoes, garlic, onion, peanut butter, plantain, and toasted peanuts. Blend for 7 minutes, until smooth and thick.

5. Pour the blended paste into a soup pot over medium heat. Add the broth and chocolate and whisk for 8 to 10 minutes, until the chocolate is melted. Season with the cumin, cinnamon, cloves, and bouillon. Stir and taste. Add salt as needed. Stir in the sesame seeds. Whisk again and let simmer for 20 minutes.

6. Remove the skin from the chicken and add the chicken to the mole sauce. Cover the pot and warm the chicken over low heat for 10 minutes. Mole is a thick sauce, but add more chicken broth if needed.

7. Serve with a side of Mexican rice, frijoles de olla, and warm corn tortillas. You can also sprinkle some toasted sesame seeds on top of the chicken.

TIP

Mole sauce freezes well. It is not a spicy sauce, but if you prefer it with a kick, add 1 or 2 dried chipotles. You can use chicken breasts instead of a whole chicken. The chicken broth is better homemade, but canned broth is a suitable replacement for precooked, oven-roasted chicken. Mole can be served with turkey, too, and used for making enmoladas or enchiladas.

ENCACAHUATADO DE POLLO
CHICKEN IN PEANUT SAUCE

Origin: Veracruz and Oaxaca | Prep time: 15 minutes | Cook time: 1 hour 20 minutes
Serves 4 | Special equipment: blender

In Oaxaca and Veracruz, this dish is part of the daily menu, but it is a menu option for special occasions, too. Chicken is the protein of choice; however, in Veracruz, home cooks prepare it with pork. And in Mexico City, some like to use beef skirt. All options are delicious. This complex, rich sauce is nearly as popular as mole poblano.

For the chicken

4 skinless chicken breasts or thighs

½ white onion

2 garlic cloves

3 celery stalks, including leaves

1 mint sprig

1 tablespoon chicken bouillon

6 cups water

For the sauce

2 tablespoons cooking oil, divided

2 garlic cloves

½ white onion

3 ancho chiles, stemmed and seeded

1 chipotle pepper, stemmed and seeded

2 cups water

4 Roma tomatoes, roasted and peeled

3 tablespoons sesame seeds, toasted

1½ cups peanuts, roasted

1½ cups chicken stock

Pinch allspice

Pinch ground cloves

½ teaspoon freshly ground black pepper

½ teaspoon cinnamon

½ teaspoon cumin

1 tablespoon chicken bouillon

Salt (optional)

Cooked rice, for serving

Cooked pinto beans, for serving

Homemade Corn Tortillas (page 22), for serving

To make the chicken

1. In a medium soup pot over low heat, combine the chicken, onion, garlic, celery, mint, bouillon, and water. Cover and cook for 45 minutes. Reserve the broth.

To make the sauce

2. In a sauté pan, heat 1 tablespoon of oil over medium heat and fry the garlic and onion for 5 to 8 minutes. Set aside. In the same oil, fry the ancho chiles and chipotle pepper for 2 minutes or less. It is crucial to avoid burning the chiles and pepper, as they can turn bitter. Turn off the heat and add the water. Soak the chiles and pepper for 10 minutes, or until soft. Reserve the soaking water.

3. Transfer the chiles and pepper to a blender with the tomatoes, garlic-onion mixture, sesame seeds, and peanuts. Blend, adding just enough reserved soaking water or chicken broth to create a smooth sauce.

4. In a sauté pan, heat the remaining 1 tablespoon of oil over medium heat and fry the allspice, cloves, black pepper, cinnamon, and cumin for 1 minute. Then pour in the peanut sauce, stir, and cook for 5 minutes. Add the bouillon and keep stirring to keep the sauce from sticking. Taste and add salt (if using).

5. Reduce the heat to low. Add the chicken, cover, and simmer for 10 minutes. Serve with a side of rice or pinto beans and enjoy with warm tortillas.

TIP
For more flavorful chicken, poach it in chicken broth with herbs. Other options include adding cooked potatoes, chayote, or zucchini. The peanut sauce works well with pork butt, ribs, or a leaner cut. Cook the pork in an Instant Pot for 45 minutes and incorporate it into the sauce.

PIPIÁN ROJO CON PAVO
RED PIPIÁN WITH TURKEY

Origin: Mexico | Prep time: 30 minutes | Cook time: 1 hour 5 minutes | Serves 6
Special equipment: Instant Pot or pressure cooker, food processor or blender

This dish is an ode to my pre-Hispanic roots, as it uses all the ingredients that were locally available before the Spanish conquest. Pipián was the Aztec Emperor Moctezuma's favorite dish and was called "totolin patzcalmollo." The main ingredient is pepita and dried chiles, and the sauce can be green or red, depending on the type of tomatoes and chiles used. Every time my mom made pipián at home, it was like a feast.

For the turkey

1 pound turkey tenderloin

½ white onion

2 garlic cloves

2 carrots, peeled and halved

3 celery sticks, including leaves

3 bay leaves

3 thyme sprigs

1 tablespoon chicken bouillon

4 cups water

For the pipián sauce

2 ancho chiles, stemmed and seeded

4 guajillo chiles, stemmed and seeded

2 chipotle peppers, stemmed and seeded

1½ cups hot water

3 Roma tomatoes, roasted and peeled

2 garlic cloves, roasted

½ white onion, roasted

3 slices baguette, fried, or ⅓ cup toasted croutons

1½ cups pepitas, roasted

4 tablespoons sesame seeds, toasted

1 tablespoon cooking oil

Pinch allspice

Pinch ground cloves

½ teaspoon freshly ground black pepper

½ teaspoon cinnamon

½ teaspoon cumin

2 cups turkey broth

1 tablespoon chicken bouillon

Salt (optional)

Cooked white rice, for serving

Homemade Corn Tortillas (page 22), for serving

To cook the turkey

1. Combine the turkey, onion, garlic, carrots, celery, bay leaves, thyme, bouillon, and water in an Instant Pot or pressure cooker. Seal the lid and cook for 15 to 20 minutes on high. Perform a quick release. Remove and set aside the turkey and reserve the broth.

To make the pipián sauce

2. In a medium bowl, soak the ancho chiles, guajillo chiles, and chipotle peppers in the hot water for 10 to 15 minutes, until softened. Reserve 1½ cups of the soaking water.

3. Transfer the chiles and peppers to a food processor or blender. Add the tomatoes, garlic, onion, bread, pepitas, sesame seeds, and reserved soaking water and process for 4 to 6 minutes, until smooth.

4. In a sauté pan, heat the oil over low heat. Add the allspice, cloves, black pepper, cinnamon, and cumin and fry for 1 minute, then pour in the sauce. Add the broth and bouillon. This sauce is thick and smooth, but if it is too thick, add more water or broth. Cook the sauce for 15 minutes, stirring. Taste and add salt (if using).

5. Thickly slice the turkey and add it to the sauce. Cover and simmer over low heat for 15 minutes. Serve the pipián with a side of white rice and warm tortillas.

VARIATION
Replace the tomatoes with 6 tomatillos and the dried chiles with 3 serrano or jalapeño peppers to make a green pipián. Try it with chicken or pork. Bulk it up with chayote or round zucchini.

ALBÓNDIGAS DE RES AL CHIPOTLE
MEXICAN BEEF MEATBALLS WITH CHIPOTLE

Origin: Mexico | Prep time: 30 minutes | Cook time: 15 minutes | Serves 6
Special equipment: blender

Albóndigas are a staple in many households. At my great-grandmother's home, this dish was part of the weekly menu. Mexican cuisine is all about layering flavors, and these chipotle meatballs are a great example of this fact. Each bite is full of flavor, and the chipotle-tomato broth delights the senses.

For the meatballs

1 slice white bread

¼ cup milk

1 egg

1 garlic clove

1 pound lean ground beef

1 teaspoon beef bouillon

1 teaspoon ground cumin

1 teaspoon freshly ground black pepper

½ cup finely chopped white onion

½ cup finely chopped cilantro
(or parsley)

For the sauce

4 cups tomato puree

½ onion, roasted

2 garlic cloves, roasted

2 canned chipotles in adobo

2½ cups beef broth or water

1 teaspoon cooking oil

1 tablespoon beef bouillon

Salt (optional)

Freshly ground black pepper (optional)

Mayocoba Refried Beans (page 111),
for serving

Cooked rice, for serving

To make the meatballs

1. In a blender, combine the bread, milk, egg, and garlic. Blend for 5 minutes, until smooth.

2. Transfer the blended mixture to a medium bowl. Add the beef, bouillon, cumin, black pepper, onion, and cilantro and mix well with your hands.

3. Using a teaspoon or small ice-cream scoop, make small meatballs
(1.5 inches). Set them on a plate and cover with plastic. Refrigerate until ready to use.

To make the sauce

4. In a blender, combine the tomato puree, onion, garlic, chipotles, and broth and blend for 5 minutes, until thoroughly mixed.

5. In a pot, heat the oil over medium heat. Pour the sauce into the pot, season it with the bouillon, and simmer for 5 minutes. Taste and add salt and black pepper (if using). Add the meatballs to the sauce, one at a time, cover, and cook for 10 minutes.

6. Serve with a side of refried beans and rice.

VARIATION

Meatballs are typically made with beef, but try using ground chicken or turkey or combine the beef with pork. For economy, some cooks add chopped hardboiled eggs or rice to the beef. Add more or fewer chipotles according to your taste. Albóndigas are freezer friendly; prepare them in advance and store them in an airtight container.

PICADILLO DE RES
BEEF PICADILLO

Origin: Mexico | Prep time: 15 minutes | Cook time: 35 minutes | Serves 4

Picadillo is a humble dish served in many homes all over Mexico. Each region has its own way of making it. Some add potatoes, peas, and carrots, whereas others include chayote, zucchini, and corn. Everyone uses ground beef or pork and all the ingredients are cut into small pieces, which is why the dish is called "picadillo."

1 tablespoon cooking oil

1 white onion, finely chopped

2 garlic cloves, minced

1 pound ground beef

1 tablespoon beef bouillon or salt

1 serrano or jalapeño pepper, chopped

2 Roma tomatoes, diced

1 cup tomato puree

½ cup beef broth or water

1½ cups frozen mix with peas and carrots

¼ cup freshly chopped cilantro

Cooked rice, for serving

Mayocoba Refried Beans (page 111), for serving

1. In a sauté pan, heat the oil over medium heat and fry the onion and garlic for 5 minutes.

2. Add the beef and cook for 15 minutes, breaking it up with a wooden spatula. Season it with the bouillon and continue cooking.

3. Add the pepper, tomatoes, and tomato puree and cook for another 5 minutes. Add the broth and frozen vegetables, cover, and cook for 10 minutes.

4. Add the cilantro and serve with rice or refried beans.

TIP
Use this beef picadillo for tacos, empanadas, sopes, or tostadas.

VARIATION
Try ground chicken, turkey, pork, or vegetarian crumbles in place of the beef. The veggies can be replaced with potatoes or other options such as mushrooms and bell peppers.

MILANESA DE RES
BEEF MILANESA

Origin: Mexico | Prep time: 15 minutes | Cook time: 30 minutes | Serves 4

Milanesas came from Europe. Bartolomeo Scappi created the first milanesa in the 16th century and served it to the pope. The dish was adopted by many and brought to Latin America and Mexico.

1 egg

¼ cup milk

Pinch salt

½ teaspoon freshly ground black pepper, plus pinch

4 thin beef steaks (see tip)

1 cup panko bread crumbs

1 tablespoon beef bouillon

½ teaspoon garlic powder

1 cup cooking oil or peanut oil

1. In a large bowl, whisk the egg, milk, salt, and ½ teaspoon black pepper for 1 to 2 minutes. Add the steaks and marinate for 5 minutes, making sure they are covered with the batter.

2. Pour the bread crumbs onto a plate and mix with the bouillon, garlic powder, and remaining pinch of black pepper. Coat each steak on both sides and set aside.

3. In a deep pan, heat the oil to over medium-high heat until hot, and fry each milanesa for 3 to 4 minutes per side, until golden brown. Use paper towels to remove excess oil and serve.

TIP

Make sure to buy tender beef cuts, such as top round. Ask the butcher to slice the steaks thin and tenderize them. Many Mexican food stores sell Mexican-style meat cuts. Look for one in your area. Many supermarkets also offer butcher services. You can transform this dish into a torta de milanesa (a sandwich using a bolillo or baguette) or serve it over a bed of greens. These milanesas also pair well with Mexican Rice (page 108), black beans, a fresh salad, creamy mashed potatoes, or French fries.

SALPICÓN DE RES
BEEF SALPICÓN

Origin: Yucatán, Tabasco, Tamaulipas, Veracruz, Mexico City, and Chiapas
Prep time: 15 minutes | Cook time: 45 minutes | Serves 4 to 6
Special equipment: Instant Pot or pressure cooker

This recipe first appeared in 16th-century Spain. It was created to repurpose meat leftovers. In Mexico, this cold dish is popular during the hot weather months. It uses skirt steak and a variety of raw vegetables, drizzled with a mustard vinaigrette. A pressure cooker is essential for preparing this dish.

For the meat

1 pound skirt steak

½ white onion

3 garlic cloves

2 bay leaves

2 whole allspice berries

3 whole black peppercorns or ⅓ teaspoon freshly ground black pepper

1 tablespoon beef bouillon or salt

6 cups water

For the vinaigrette

1 tablespoon whole-grain mustard

Juice of 1 lime

¼ cup apple cider vinegar

1 teaspoon salt

1 teaspoon freshly ground black pepper

1 teaspoon Mexican oregano

1 cup extra-virgin olive oil

For the salad

4 cups shredded romaine lettuce

2 cups diced Roma tomatoes

½ red onion, cut into thin rounds

4 radishes, cut into thin rounds

1 avocado, sliced

¼ cup cilantro leaves

To make the meat

1. Combine the steak, onion, garlic, bay leaves, allspice, peppercorns, and bouillon in a pressure cooker. Pour in the water. Seal the cooker and cook on high for 45 minutes. Allow the pressure to release naturally.

2. Remove the meat while it's still warm. Using two forks, shred the meat, then transfer it to an airtight container and refrigerate. Reserve the beef broth for later use.

To make the vinaigrette

3. In a small bowl, combine the mustard, lime juice, vinegar, salt, black pepper, and oregano and whisk for 1 minute.

4. Incorporate the oil slowly, while whisking, to emulsify the vinaigrette.

To make the salad

5. In a large bowl, use two forks to combine the meat with ½ cup of vinaigrette. Add the lettuce and gently toss the salad.

6. Serve the meat and lettuce garnished with the tomatoes, onion, radishes, avocado, and cilantro and drizzled with more vinaigrette.

TIP

Salpicón is perfect for an informal gathering or outdoor activity. Pair the salpicón with tostadas or chips and serve it as an appetizer. Serve with queso fresco and a side of pickled carrots and jalapeño slices.

CARNE ASADA
BEEF ASADA

Origin: Nuevo León, Sonora, and Mexico | Prep time: 10 minutes, plus 45 minutes to marinate | Cook time: 20 minutes | Serves 6
Special equipment: charcoal grill

In North Mexico, Sundays are for parrilladas with the family, and carne asada is the star of the menu. It is a time when families socialize and create memories while enjoying juicy steaks. Most homes have a charcoal grill built into the backyard. The meat marinates for hours and all the side dishes are prepared fresh while the meat cooks—a true tradition of good food and togetherness.

⅓ cup lime juice

½ cup blonde beer

1 tablespoon coarse sea salt

1 teaspoon freshly ground black pepper

1 teaspoon ground cumin

3 tablespoons corn oil

3 garlic cloves, chopped

6 New York steaks, cut thin

12 scallions

4 jalapeño peppers

2 limes, quartered

Ranchero Beans (page 112), for serving

Homemade Corn Tortillas (page 22), for serving

Grilled Guacamole (page 31), for serving

Pico de Gallo Salsa (page 26), for serving

1. In a large bowl, whisk together the lime juice, beer, salt, black pepper, and cumin. Whisk in the oil gradually and whisk for 5 minutes to emulsify. Incorporate the garlic and set aside.

2. Drench the meat in the large bowl of marinade, cover it with plastic wrap, and refrigerate for 30 to 45 minutes.

3. Preheat the charcoal grill to 400°F.

4. Remove the steaks from the marinade and grill for 3 minutes per side, until well seared and showing grill marks. Set aside to let rest for 2 minutes before slicing.

5. Grill the scallions and jalapeños for 10 minutes and place them in a small bowl with the limes.

6. Slice the steaks and serve with the scallion-jalapeño mixture, ranchero beans, warm tortillas, guacamole, and pico de gallo.

LOMO DE CERDO EN SALSA DE CIRUELAS CON CHIPOTLE
PORK IN PRUNE-CHIPOTLE SAUCE

Origin: Chiapas and Mexico | Prep time: 20 minutes | Cook time: 50 minutes | Serves 6

This simple to prepare but celebratory dish has been enjoyed as a Christmas staple for generations in many households. The sweetness and spiciness of the sauce is the perfect marriage with the pork. This dish pairs well with a salad or creamy spaghetti pasta.

10 prunes, pitted

1½ cups hot water

2 canned chipotles in adobo

2 garlic cloves, roasted

1 teaspoon dried cumin

1 teaspoon dried Mexican oregano

1 teaspoon freshly ground black pepper

1 tablespoon chicken bouillon

1 teaspoon butter

1 pound pork loin

1. Preheat the oven to 375°F.

2. Soak the prunes in the hot water for 10 minutes, or until plumped. Transfer them to a blender with 1 cup of the prune soaking water, the chipotles, garlic, cumin, oregano, black pepper, and bouillon. Blend until smooth.

3. Butter a rectangular baking pan and add the pork loin. Pour the sauce over top of the pork. Cover the pan with aluminum foil.

4. Bake the pork loin for 45 minutes. Remove the foil and broil the meat on low for 5 to 7 minutes, or until it reaches an internal temperature of 150°F.

5. Let the pork rest before thinly slicing and serving.

VARIATION
You can omit the chipotles or replace them with 2 guajillo chiles or 2 ancho chiles. This sauce also pairs well with turkey tenderloin and chicken breasts.

CERDO EN ADOBO
PORK ADOBO

Origin: Puebla, Jalisco, Hidalgo, Tamaulipas, Oaxaca, Zacatecas, and Campeche
Prep time: 15 minutes | Cook time: 1 hour | Serves 6
Special equipment: blender, Instant Pot or pressure cooker

When looking for something comforting, I think about the flavors and smells coming out of my mom's kitchen, and adobo is one of those dishes that take me home. Adobo is a dried pepper sauce made with guajillo and ancho chiles. Depending on the state, there are subtle differences in the chile mixes and spices. However, all Mexican adobos are exceptional.

4 guajillo chiles, stemmed and seeded

2 ancho chiles, stemmed and seeded

2 cups hot water

1 white onion, roasted

2 small Roma tomatoes, roasted and peeled

3 garlic cloves, roasted

1 pound pork loin, cut into chunks

1 teaspoon salt

1 teaspoon freshly ground black pepper

1 tablespoon corn oil

2 tablespoons apple cider vinegar

1 teaspoon ground cumin

1 teaspoon dried Mexican oregano

1 tablespoon chicken bouillon

1 pound new potatoes, peeled and cooked (optional)

Cooked Mexican Rice (page 108), for serving

Frijoles de la olla, for serving

1. Soak the guajillo and ancho chiles in the hot water for 10 to 15 minutes, until softened. Reserve all the chile soaking water. Transfer the chiles, 1 cup of the soaking water, onion, tomatoes, and garlic to a blender. Blend for 3 to 5 minutes, until the adobo sauce is smooth.

2. Season the pork with the salt and black pepper and set aside. Set the pressure cooker to the "Sauté" mode. Pour in the oil and sear the pork for 3 minutes. Add the blended adobo sauce, vinegar, cumin, oregano, and bouillon. Stir in an additional 1 cup of chile soaking water.

3. Seal the cooker and cook on high for 45 minutes. Perform a natural release and add the potatoes (if using). Set the pressure cooker to "Sauté" and simmer for 5 to 7 minutes.

4. Serve the pork adobo with red Mexican rice (page 108) and frijoles de la olla.

CHICHARRÓN DE CERDO EN SALSA VERDE

PORK CHICHARRÓN IN GREEN SAUCE

Origin: Mexico | Prep time: 15 minutes | Cook time: 25 minutes | Serves 4
Special equipment: blender

Chicharróns are pork cracklings that are typically enjoyed as snacks or in tacos. Fresh chicharróns are available every Sunday, but if they are not eaten the same day, they are repurposed by cooking them with a green tomatillo sauce. Tomatillos and peppers are part of the indigenous legacy, whereas we inherited pork from Spain. This dish is a true example of the mix of cultures, and this humble dish has been a staple of Mexican cuisine for many years.

1 (16-ounce) can cooked tomatillos

2 jalapeño peppers, roasted

2 garlic cloves, roasted

½ cup water

⅓ cup fresh cilantro leaves

1 tablespoon cooking oil

1 tablespoon chicken bouillon

Salt (optional)

1 pound chicharróns, cut into medium pieces

1. In a blender, combine the tomatillos, jalapeños, garlic, water, and cilantro. Blend until smooth.

2. In a soup pot, heat the oil over medium heat and cook the tomatillo sauce 5 minutes. Season with the bouillon and simmer for 15 minutes. Taste and add salt (if using). Add the chicharróns, cook for 5 minutes, and serve.

TIP
Adding leftover carnitas to the dish makes it even tastier. Fresh tomatillos are preferable, but canned are a convenient option without compromising the authentic flavor. For a spicier sauce, add 2 chiles de árbol. Serve this dish with black beans and Homemade Corn Tortillas (page 22).

TAMALES DE CERDO
PORK TAMALES

Origin: Mexico | Prep time: 1 hour | Cook time: 1 hour 50 minutes | Makes 20 tamales
Special equipment: blender, Instant Pot or pressure cooker, electric mixer, tamalera

Tamales are a must-have for Christmas, Three Kings Day, and Día de la Candelaria. Tamales come in different varieties, but my favorite is red pork tamales. These tamales showcase the mix of cultures using indigenous ingredients such as corn, chiles, and pork thanks to the Spanish legacy. Making tamales is labor intensive and a work of love, but it is so worth it, especially when enjoyed with a cup of Mexican hot chocolate.

For the guajillo sauce

8 guajillo chiles, seeded and stemmed

1 cup hot water

2 garlic cloves

1 teaspoon cooking oil

1 teaspoon ground cumin

1 teaspoon Mexican oregano

½ tablespoon chicken bouillon or salt

For the meat

1 tablespoon cooking oil

1 pound pork butt, cut into chunks

1 teaspoon ground cumin

1 teaspoon dried oregano

1 cube chicken bouillon

For the masa

3 cups masa harina

1 teaspoon salt, plus 1 tablespoon

2½ cups warm water

1⅓ cups pork lard or vegetable shortening, at room temperature

1 teaspoon baking powder

2 cups chicken broth

20 corn husks, at least 4 inches wide, soaked and ready to use

To make the guajillo sauce

1. In a saucepan, soak the chiles in the hot water for 15 minutes, or until soft. Transfer the chiles, 1 cup of chile soaking water, and garlic to a blender. Blend for 5 minutes into a smooth paste. Strain the paste to get a velvety consistency.

2. In another saucepan, heat the oil over low heat and pour in the guajillo sauce. Whisk in the cumin, oregano, and bouillon. Cook for 10 minutes. Set aside to cool.

To cook the meat

3. In a pressure cooker set to the "Sauté" mode, heat the oil and fry the pork for 7 to 10 minutes, until seared.

4. Season with the cumin, oregano, and bouillon. Stir in 3 cups of the guajillo sauce.

5. Seal the lid and cook on high for 45 minutes. Perform a quick release and shred the pork. Set aside to cool.

To make the masa

6. Combine the masa harina and 1 teaspoon of salt in a medium bowl and use your hands to mix together. Add the warm water slowly to start hydrating the masa. Work the dough with your hands until it feels smooth and soft, like Play-Doh.

7. In an electric mixer, beat the lard with the baking powder for 1 to 2 minutes, until light and fluffy. Still beating, add the masa in three parts. Then, add the broth and the remaining 1 tablespoon of salt.

8. Test the consistency of the dough by dropping a dollop in a glass of cold water. If the dough floats, the masa is ready.

9. Make one tamale at a time. Take a few corn husks at a time; shake off the water. Place the corn husk in the palm of your hand with the wide side closest to you. Spread 3 tablespoons of masa all over the bottom half of the husk. Add 2 tablespoons of pork filling lengthwise down the center of the tamale. Fold one side first, then the other side. Fold the empty top section down.

10. Fill the bottom of the tamalera with water and insert the steamer basket. Arrange the tamales, open-side up, on the steamer basket inside the tamalera. Cover the tamales with a cloth or more corn husks to keep them moist during the cooking process. Cook the tamales for 45 minutes to 1 hour. Check the tamalera and add more hot water to the steamer if necessary.

ENCHILADAS MINERAS
MINER ENCHILADAS

Origin: Guanajuato | Prep time: 15 minutes | Cook time: 30 minutes | Serves 4

The name of this dish comes from the fact that Guanajuato became the world's leading silver mine in the 18th century. Miners would go home after a long day of work to enjoy these homemade, hearty enchiladas. In this version, the tortillas are dipped in the guajillo sauce and then fried.

For the guajillo sauce

8 guajillos chiles, seeded and stemmed

2 cups hot water

2 garlic cloves

1 teaspoon cooking oil

1 teaspoon ground cumin

½ teaspoon Mexican oregano

1 tablespoon chicken bouillon

For the enchiladas

2 tablespoons cooking oil, plus 12 teaspoons, for frying

3 boiled potatoes, peeled and diced

4 cooked carrots, peeled and diced

12 corn tortillas

1 cup crumbled Ranchero queso fresco

2 cups shredded romaine lettuce

4 pickled jalapeño peppers

To make the guajillo sauce

1. In a small bowl, soak the chiles in the hot water for 10 minutes, or until soft. Transfer the chiles, 1½ cups of chile soaking water, and the garlic to a blender. Blend on high into a paste.

2. In a saucepan, heat the oil over low heat. Pour in the guajillo sauce and cook for 3 minutes. Add the cumin, oregano, and bouillon. Stir and simmer for 5 minutes. Set aside.

To make the enchiladas

3. In a skillet, heat 2 tablespoons of oil over medium heat and sauté the potatoes and carrots for 7 to 10 minutes. Transfer to a medium bowl and set aside.

4. In the same skillet, heat 1 teaspoon of oil. Dip the corn tortillas, one at a time, into the guajillo sauce, then fry in the skillet for 1 minute on each side. Repeat with the remaining tortillas and oil.

5. Place the tortillas on a serving plate and top them with some of the cheese. Roll each tortilla or close them into half-moons.

6. Top the enchiladas with the potatoes and carrots, lettuce, and more cheese. Serve with the pickled jalapeños.

TIP

The potatoes, carrots, and guajillo sauce can be cooked ahead of time. Use yellow corn tortillas, which tend to be stronger than white.

VARIATION

In Mexico City, enchiladas have requesón (a Mexican ricotta cheese mixed with chopped epazote) and are served with ribbons of Mexican crema and avocado slices rather than cooked vegetables.

CHILES RELLENOS
STUFFED POBLANO PEPPERS

Origin: Puebla | Prep time: 15 minutes | Cook time: 30 minutes | Serves 4
Special equipment: blender

I have never met anyone who doesn't enjoy a good chile relleno. These stuffed poblano peppers were part of my family's traditional menu for Lent or celebratory meals. Many happy memories come to my mind with this recipe, which was created by the nuns of the Santa Mónica Convent in Puebla, making it an icon of Mexican cuisine.

For the tomato sauce

8 Roma tomatoes, steamed, peeled, and seeded

¼ cup water

1 tablespoon chicken bouillon or salt

1 teaspoon sugar

1 teaspoon freshly ground black pepper

1 teaspoon cooking oil

½ onion, cut into rounds

For the stuffed peppers

4 large poblano peppers, roasted, peeled, seeded, and deveined

2½ cups shredded Chihuahua cheese, or Monterey Jack

1 cup wheat flour

4 large eggs, separated

1 cup frying oil

Mexican Rice (page 108), for serving

To make the tomato sauce

1. In a blender, combine the tomatoes, water, bouillon, sugar, and black pepper. Blend on high for 3 minutes, until pureed.

2. In a skillet, heat the oil over medium heat and fry the onion for 2 to 3 minutes, until translucent.

3. Pour the tomato puree into the skillet and simmer for another 10 minutes. Keep warm.

To make the stuffed peppers

4. Stuff the peppers with the cheese and roll them in the flour. Secure the stuffed and coated peppers with wooden toothpicks. Set on a plate and set aside.

5. In a small bowl, whip the egg whites for 5 minutes, until peaks form. Add the yolks, one at a time, and continue whipping until soft, yellow, and fluffy.

6. In a skillet, heat the oil to 175ºF. Test the temperature by adding a dollop of batter. If it fries fast, the oil is ready to use.

7. Working one pepper at a time, dip a pepper in the batter and drop it into the hot oil. Fry on both sides for 3 to 5 minutes, until golden brown. Transfer the fried pepper to a paper towel–lined plate to remove excess oil. Repeat with the remaining stuffed peppers.

8. Serve the stuffed peppers with warm tomato sauce and a side of Mexican rice.

TIP

Prepare the tomato sauce and prep the peppers the night before. The batter might require more than 4 eggs, depending on their size. Replace the shredded cheese with refried beans, veggies, ground beef, or any other combination of your choice. Roasting the poblanos can be intimidating, but do not fret. See page 18 for instructions.

CHORIZO DE CERDO CASERO
HOMEMADE PORK CHORIZO

Origin: Mexico | Prep time: 2 hours 45 minutes | Makes 3 rolls
Special equipment: blender, food processor, cheesecloth

Mexican chorizo differs from the classic Spanish chorizo as it is made with raw pork, whereas the Spanish version is usually aged and smoked. Mexican chorizo first appeared 400 years ago in Toluca, where nowadays there are many chorizo styles such as the famous chorizo verde and the longaniza. Making your own chorizo is fun and easy.

For the sauce

6 guajillo chiles, stemmed and seeded

2 pasilla chiles, stemmed and seeded

4 cascabel chiles, stemmed and seeded

2 cups hot water

3 garlic cloves, roasted

½ white onion, roasted

1 teaspoon Mexican oregano

1 teaspoon dried marjoram

½ teaspoon dried thyme

1 tablespoon ground cumin

1 teaspoon ground cloves

1 teaspoon freshly ground black pepper

2 tablespoons smoked paprika

1 tablespoon hickory-smoked salt

½ cup apple cider vinegar

1 tablespoon chicken bouillon

For the chorizo

2 pounds ground pork

1 cup chopped smoked bacon

To make the sauce

1. In a saucepan, soak the guajillo, pasilla, and cascabel chiles in the hot water for 15 minutes, until softened. Transfer the chiles, ½ cup of the chile soaking water, garlic, onion, oregano, marjoram, thyme, cumin, cloves, pepper, paprika, hickory-smoked salt, vinegar, and bouillon to a blender. Blend for 5 to 7 minutes into a paste. Transfer the paste to an airtight container and refrigerate.

To make the chorizo

2. Add the ground pork and bacon to a food processor and process until completely combined. You may have to do this twice for a finer finish.

3. Transfer the mixture to a large bowl and combine it with the sauce. Use food-grade gloves and mix with your hands for 10 to 15 minutes, until fully integrated.

4. Wrap the chorizo in cheesecloth and strain to remove any excess water. Refrigerate the chorizo in the colander for 1 to 2 hours. The mixture should be dry enough before making the chorizo rolls.

5. Cut three sheets of plastic wrap. Lay out one sheet and add one-third of the chorizo. Roll tightly and close on both sides. Repeat twice more.

6. Place the chorizo rolls in a sealed container and store in the freezer until ready to enjoy.

TIP

To save time, ask the butcher to mix the bacon with the ground pork. Cook the chorizo with pork lard and use it for making tacos, Mexican Chorizo with Eggs (page 41), sopes, and much more.

SIDES AND SALADS

ARROZ ROJO A LA MEXICANA
MEXICAN RICE

Origin: Mexico and Guerrero | Prep time: 30 minutes | Cook time: 40 minutes | Serves 6

The Spaniards brought rice to America. In Mexico, rice became an essential part of the culinary culture, as it is considered a symbol of fertility. Jojutla de Juárez is the home for Morelos rice, which doesn't release starch and remains firm when cooked. All Mexican households have consumed this rice since the late 1800s. Rice in Mexico can be white, red, or green, but red Mexican rice is a staple served with many favorite dishes such as mole and enchiladas.

2 cups long-grain rice

2 tablespoons cooking oil

2 whole serrano peppers

2 garlic cloves

1 cup Mexican-style tomato sauce

1 cube chicken bouillon

1 teaspoon salt

1 teaspoon freshly ground black pepper

2½ cups warm water

1 bunch fresh cilantro

1 cup frozen peas and carrots

1. Rinse the rice with cold water and set aside to dry in a colander. Mexican cooks leave it near a sunny window for about 30 minutes.

2. In a medium skillet or rice pot, heat the oil over medium heat and fry the rice for 7 minutes, until toasty. Reduce the heat to low.

3. Add the peppers and garlic and sauté for 2 minutes. Add the tomato sauce, bouillon, salt, and pepper and stir gently. Add the water and cilantro and cook, covered, for 15 to 20 minutes. Do not be tempted to stir. If the rice needs more water, add a few drops, but not too much or else the rice will be too soft.

4. Add the carrots and peas and replace the lid. Cook for 7 to 10 minutes. Turn off the heat and leave the rice covered until ready to serve.

TIP

Rinsing the rice removes the starch and prevents it from sticking together and becoming mushy when cooked, so do not skip this step. Frying the rice is the secret for obtaining the authentic flavor. Frying also prevents the rice from sticking together. Long-grain rice is closer to Morelos rice, which is not sold in the United States. For every cup of rice, you will need 2 cups of liquid. Make sure the water is warm for even cooking.

MEXICAN INDIGENOUS VEGETABLES AND FRUITS

The pre-Hispanic diet was mainly vegetarian. The Maya grew maize, beans, and squash in milpas, small pieces of land. In the great Tenochtitlan, Mexicans grew their crops on man-made islands known as chinampas in Lake Texcoco. Aside from beans, chayote squash, chiles, and maize, Mesoamerican indigenous groups grew cacao, amaranth, chia, peanuts, vanilla, sweet potato, nopales and cactus fruits, pitaya, agave, avocados, tomatoes, papaya, jícama, nance, zapote fruit varieties, tomatoes, mango Ataulfo, bananas, cherimoya, tomatillos, and pineapple.

Olmec, Teotihuacan, Zapotec, Huastec, Mixtec, Otomi, Totonac, Mazahua, and Aztec cooking techniques are present in dishes we eat today. Good examples are crafting hot sauces, roasting over direct flame, steaming tamales, and the boiling method for vegetables and cacti. Hot and cold drinks prepared with cacao were mostly enjoyed by the upper classes. Nowadays, the inclusion of insects as a good source of protein is thanks to these indigenous groups, who introduced us to chapulines, jumiles, chinicuiles, and escamoles. And let us not forget the Aztecs' uses of corn to make pozole, atoles, and champurrados, and the Mayas' discovery of nixtamalization, still used to process corn.

ARROZ VERDE DE CHILE POBLANO
GREEN POBLANO RICE

Origin: Puebla | Prep time: 30 minutes | Cook time: 30 minutes | Serves 4
Special equipment: food processor, rice pot

Green rice is prepared by families that live in Central Mexico. This kind of rice is not commonly found on restaurant menus. Sometimes, it is served with crumbled cheese and Mexican crema; it is also made white and with roasted poblano peppers and corn kernels—a tasty side for grilled chicken or steak.

1 cup long-grain rice

2 large poblano peppers, seeded, stemmed, and deveined

¼ white onion

2 garlic cloves

½ cup cilantro leaves

2 cups water, at room temperature, divided

1 tablespoon cooking oil

1 tablespoon chicken bouillon or sea salt

1 cup frozen or fresh corn kernels

1. Rinse the rice with cold water (do not soak) and dry in a colander for about 30 minutes.

2. In a food processor, combine the peppers, onion, garlic, cilantro, and ½ cup of water. Process to a green puree.

3. In a rice pot, heat the oil over high heat and fry the rice for 3 minutes, until well coated. Do not brown.

4. Reduce the heat to medium and stir in the green puree and bouillon. Cook for 2 to 3 minutes without stirring. Add the remaining 1½ cups of water. Cover and cook for 15 minutes.

5. Add the corn. Replace the lid and cook for another 5 minutes. If the rice needs more water, add a few drops but not too much or else the rice will be too soft. Turn off the heat and leave the rice covered until ready to serve.

VARIATION

Preparing white rice with roasted poblano pepper strips and corn kernels uses the same method as this recipe but omits the chicken bouillon. The poblanos must be roasted, peeled, seeded, deveined, julienned, and added with the corn in step 5. Both versions are very tasty and pair well with crumbled Ranchero queso fresco and Mexican crema.

FRIJOLES MAYOS REFRITOS
MAYOCOBA REFRIED BEANS

Origin: Mexico | Prep time: 15 minutes | Cook time: 1 hour | Serves 8
Special equipment: Instant Pot

1 pound dry Mayocoba beans

6 cups water

2 tablespoons salt

1 large garlic clove

½ white onion

2 bay leaves

1 whole chile de árbol (optional)

1 tablespoon pork lard

1. In an Instant Pot, combine the beans, water, salt, garlic, onion, bay leaves, and chile de árbol (if using). Seal the lid and cook on high for 45 minutes. Allow the pressure to release naturally. Using a slotted spoon, remove 2 cups of beans.

2. In a skillet, melt the lard over medium heat. Add the beans and mash them into a puree.

3. Reduce the heat to low and allow the beans to become a paste, stirring continuously to avoid the beans sticking to the skillet.

4. Serve in a medium bowl.

TIP

Home cooks in Mexico soak the dry beans the night before, because they use a clay pot instead of a pressure cooker and the soaking reduces the cooking time. Soaking is not necessary when using a pressure cooker. This technique works for any kind of dry bean. Try adding herbs such as epazote, cumin, oregano, marjoram, etc. When the refried beans are ready, you can add Chihuahua-style cheese for making cheesy beans or blend the beans with enough bean broth to make soup. Cotija cheese and corn chips make a great garnish for these refried beans.

FRIJOLES CHARROS
RANCHERO BEANS

Origin: Coahuila and Tamaulipas | Prep time: 15 minutes | Cook time: 30 minutes
Serves 4 | Special equipment: cast-iron soup pot

This dish gets its name from the need to feed the "charros" (Mexican cowboys) with easy, hearty meals. Cowboys used to work long hours taking care of the cattle, and they needed an inexpensive hot meal to cook outdoors; this is how the brothy bean dish became so popular in North Mexico, with a few variants depending on the state.

1 teaspoon pork lard or cooking oil

4 bacon strips, cut into small pieces

⅓ cup smoked ham, cubed (or 2 small diced hot dogs or chorizo)

½ cup diced white onion

1 teaspoon ground cumin

1 garlic clove, finely chopped

2 serrano peppers, finely chopped

1 cup diced beefsteak tomato

1 teaspoon chicken bouillon

4 cups canned pinto beans

1 cup water

1 cup blonde beer

Sea salt (optional)

⅓ cup freshly chopped cilantro

1. In a cast-iron soup pot, heat the lard over high heat and fry the bacon until golden brown. Remove some of the fat, if desired. Reduce the heat to medium, add the ham, and fry for 5 to 7 minutes.

2. Stir in the onion, cumin, garlic, and peppers and sauté for another 5 minutes. Add the tomatoes and bouillon and simmer until the tomatoes are soft.

3. Add the beans, water, and beer. Stir, cover, reduce the heat to low, and cook for 15 minutes. Taste and add salt (if using). Serve the beans hot and garnished with the cilantro.

TIP

The longer the beans simmer, the better the flavor. Try Mayocoba beans instead of pinto. Pair these beans with carne asada or garnish them with pork rinds (cueritos) and eat them as a main dish with flour tortillas.

FRIJOLES PUERCOS
DIRTY BEANS

Origin: Sinaloa, Colima, Guanajuato, Michoacán, and Nayarit | Prep time: 15 minutes
Cook time: 40 minutes | Serves 4 | Special equipment: Mexican clay
pot or cast-iron soup pot, blender

Dirty beans are a typical party appetizer. I first tried them in Acaponeta, Nayarit, at a friend's home. I was so intrigued by this dish that her mother taught me how to cook it and I became a big frijoles puercos fan. However, they are a tradition in other states, too, specifically Sinaloa, where they pride themselves on making the best dirty beans. Each region and household has their secrets on how to prepare this recipe. No matter the version, frijoles puercos are fantastic.

2 tablespoons pork lard

½ cup Homemade Pork Chorizo (page 104)

2 cups cooked Mayocoba Refried Beans (page 111) or canned

¼ cup bean broth water

1 teaspoon chipotle sauce (see steps 1 and 3 of Chicken in Creamy Chipotle Sauce, page 80), or 1 chipotle in adobo, chopped

2 tablespoons chopped pickled jalapeño peppers

¾ cup shredded Chihuahua cheese (or Monterey Jack)

Salt (optional)

Corn chips, for serving

1. In a Mexican clay pot or a cast-iron soup pot, melt the lard over high heat. Add the chorizo and fry for 10 minutes, until separated and browned.

2. In a blender, combine the beans, bean broth water, and chipotle sauce. Blend until smooth.

3. Stir the blended beans into the chorizo. Reduce the heat to medium and keep stirring to keep the beans from sticking. The beans will start bubbling and thickening after 20 minutes. Add the jalapeños and cheese. Stir again and cook for another 5 minutes.

4. When the cheese has melted and the mixture has the texture of a cheesy dip, taste and add salt (if using). Remove the beans from the heat and serve with corn chips.

ENSALADA MEXICANA DE POLLO

MEXICAN CHICKEN SALAD

Origin: Mexico | 30 Minutes or Less | Prep time: 20 minutes | Serves 6

This chicken salad is served by moms and grandmothers all over Mexico. It is a staple for parties and served during the summer as a main dish. This salad has the same ingredients as Russian potato salad, but shredded chicken is added for a more nutritious dish. Mexican chicken salad is often paired with saltines and served over a bed of lettuce with a pickled jalapeño.

½ cup mayonnaise

½ cup sour cream

Juice of ½ lime

1 teaspoon yellow mustard

1 teaspoon sea salt

½ teaspoon freshly ground black pepper

2 cups shredded chicken (white meat)

⅓ cup finely chopped celery

1 cup cooked and diced carrots

1 cup cooked peas

1 cup cooked and diced potatoes

¼ cup freshly chopped parsley

1. In a large bowl, whisk together the mayonnaise, sour cream, lime juice, mustard, salt, and pepper until creamy.

2. Add the chicken and celery and mix with a spatula. Add the carrots and peas and mix gently. Then, fold in the potatoes.

3. Serve in a large bowl, family style. Or, for a nicer presentation, use a small bowl or ramekin, add some salad, and press it down with a spoon. Place a lettuce leaf or a bed of shredded lettuce on top, turn the bowl upside-down, and unmold the salad on top of the lettuce. Garnish with the parsley and serve.

TIP

The vegetables can be frozen, but they'll need to be cooked and cooled before use. The chicken can be leftovers from the previous day, a rotisserie chicken from the store, or canned white meat.

ENSALADA DE CHAYOTE
CHAYOTE SALAD

Origin: Mexico | 30 Minutes or Less, Vegan | Prep time: 10 minutes
Cook time: 20 minutes | Serves 4

In Mexican home cooking, adding cooked vegetables to salads is widespread, especially if those vegetables are in season. Chayote is a close family member to the cucumber, so they can be eaten raw. Depending on the area, chayotes are also known as mirliton squash. This veggie tastes like a sweet zucchini with cucumber notes.

3 large chayotes

½ cup olive oil

¼ cup white vinegar

Juice of ½ lime

1 teaspoon dried Mexican oregano

1 teaspoon sea salt

1 teaspoon freshly ground black pepper

½ red onion, thinly sliced

1. In a deep soup pot, cover the chayotes with water. Bring to a boil and cook for 15 to 20 minutes. The texture has to be firm, not mushy. When the chayotes are cooked, drop them into a bowl of ice water and leave them for 10 minutes.

2. Meanwhile, in a small bowl, whisk together the oil, vinegar, lime juice, oregano, salt, and pepper until emulsified. Add the onion and let it marinate for 10 minutes.

3. Peel the chayotes, then cut them in half and then again lengthwise. Inside the chayote, there is a delicious seed. Add it to the salad. Place the chayote slices on a serving plate.

4. Spoon some of the dressing with onions on top of the chayotes. Serve with the remaining dressing on the side.

TIP

Chayotes can be eaten raw, peeled and spiralized or shredded, and drizzled with vinaigrette.

ENSALADA DE NOPALITOS
CACTUS SALAD

Origin: Mexico | Vegetarian | Prep time: 15 minutes | Cook time: 20 minutes | Serves 6

In Mexican cuisine, cactus appears in many dishes, such as nopales salad, grilled cactus with cheese and salsa, egg and pork dishes, smoothies, and even nutritional supplements. Cooked cactus is meaty with a pleasantly sour flavor. There are many varieties of nopales, all indigenous to Mexico. This cactus salad is simple to prepare and served in many homes during Lent.

4 cups cactus nopales, cut into strips as needed

1 teaspoon sea salt, plus pinch

Juice of 3 limes

2 tablespoons olive oil

1 teaspoon freshly ground black pepper

½ cup finely chopped red onion

1 cup diced tomatoes

1 jalapeño pepper, finely chopped (optional)

⅓ cup cilantro leaves

1 avocado, sliced

3 tablespoons cotija cheese

1. In a deep pot over medium heat, cover the nopal strips with water, add a pinch of salt, and cook for 20 minutes.

2. Meanwhile, in a small bowl, whisk together the lime juice, oil, the remaining 1 teaspoon of salt, and the black pepper. Set the dressing aside.

3. When the nopales are tender and meaty to the bite, remove them from the pot, rinse them with running water, then strain to remove any slime. If the cactus is still slimy, rinse and strain again.

4. Place the cooked nopales in a medium bowl and add the onion, tomatoes, and jalapeño (if using). Pour the dressing over and mix.

5. Cover and refrigerate the salad for at least 15 minutes. When ready to serve, transfer the salad to a large bowl and mix in the cilantro. Garnish with the avocado and cheese.

TIP

Adding five tomatillo skins (not the husks) or a clean copper coin to the bottom of the pot helps reduce the cactus slime.

ENSALADA DE AGUACATE
AVOCADO SALAD

Origin: Mexico | 30 Minutes or Less, Vegan | Prep time: 15 minutes | Serves 4

Avocado salad is such a simple dish to make, which is why many home cooks serve it with a variety of meals. This salad requires a firm Hass avocado and a sharp knife. Most of the avocados consumed in the United States come from Michoacán, but the crop is also grown in California and Chile.

2 large Hass avocados

Juice of 1 lime

1 tablespoon olive oil

Salt

Freshly ground black pepper

Halve the avocados lengthwise, remove the pits and the skins, and slice. Lay the slices on a plate. Drizzle the slices with the lime juice and oil. Season with salt and pepper.

TIP

Firm avocados have a deep, dark green color and, when pressed, feel firm but slightly tender. Another way to check the ripeness is by removing the stem. If the flesh looks green, the avocado is ready to use. If the color is brown, the avocado has passed its prime. Try this salad with tomatoes, sliced onions, grapefruit, and orange slices.

ENSALADA DE NAVIDAD
CHRISTMAS SALAD

Origin: Mexico | 30 Minutes or Less, Vegetarian | Prep time: 30 minutes | Serves 6

Christmastime in Mexico is a special time of the year. Several dishes are served only for the holiday, such as this colorful Christmas salad crafted with bright and flavorful seasonal fruits and veggies. Each family has their own twist for preparing this recipe, but all are fresh options that have become a deeply rooted tradition in many regions within Mexico.

¼ cup orange juice

¼ cup beet juice (or pomegranate juice)

Juice of 1 lime

1 tablespoon honey

6 to 8 romaine lettuce leaves

1 cup diced jícama

1 cup orange slices

½ cup pineapple chunks

½ cup diced Golden Delicious apple

½ cup beets, cooked and diced (or canned)

½ cup pomegranate seeds

¼ cup toasted peanuts (or honey-roasted)

2 tablespoons dried coconut shavings

1. In a small bowl, whisk together the orange juice, beet juice, lime juice, and honey. Refrigerate until ready to use.

2. On a large serving plate, lay the lettuce leaves in the shape of a flower. Add the jícama, spreading it evenly. Do the same with the orange slices, pineapple, and apple. Incorporate the beets and sprinkle with the pomegranate seeds, peanuts, and coconut.

3. Serve family style, with the dressing on the side.

TIP

This colorful salad requires precise cutting of the veggies and fruits for the best presentation. Use any other seasonal fruits, such as guavas, papaya, mandarins, or plantains. Instead of peanuts, use pecans, almonds, sesame seeds, or pine nuts. If using raw beets, cook them unpeeled in a pressure cooker for 30 minutes. Reserve the cooking water and use it instead of the beet juice for the dressing.

DESSERTS AND DRINKS

FLAN CLÁSICO DE VAINILLA CON CARAMELO

CLASSIC VANILLA FLAN WITH CARAMEL

Origin: Puebla | Vegetarian | Prep time: 15 minutes | Cook time: 1 hour 15 minutes
Serves 8 to 10 | Special equipment: flanera, blender

Flans or custards have been very popular in Europe since medieval times, and they were brought to Mexico by nuns. This particular flan recipe is my mom's. We cooked this dessert together many years back, and I learned how to make it with her guidance. See the tip for other cooking techniques. Enjoy this recipe as-is or with whipped cream and seasonal fruit.

For the caramel

6 tablespoons water, at room temperature

⅔ cup refined sugar

For the flan

4 eggs

½ cup sugar

1 (14-oz) can condensed milk

1 (12-oz) can evaporated milk

1 tablespoon vanilla extract

To make the caramel

1. In a flan pan (flanera), melt the sugar in the water over medium heat, until it becomes caramel, turning to cover the sides and bottom of the pan. Remove the flanera from the heat and let it cool. The caramel will become hard and could crack, but that is okay.

To make the flan

2. In a blender, combine the eggs, sugar, condensed milk, evaporated milk, and vanilla. Blend for 5 to 7 minutes, until the mixture is soft and yellow. Pour the mixture into the pan lined with the caramel.

3. Use a double boiler or fill a saucepan with enough water to create a water bath. Set the flanera on top and cover with the lid. Cook over low heat for 45 minutes to 1 hour, until firm. Set aside to cool.

4. When cool, refrigerate the flan for at least 12 hours before serving. To serve, unmold the flan onto a serving plate and enjoy.

TIP

The flan can be cooked in a pressure cooker, on the stove using a double boiler, or in the oven using a water bath. A classic flanera is 8-by-3 inches with a lid appropriate for a 6-quart pressure cooker. A double boiler can be used on the stovetop, or you can use an 8-by-3-inch round cake pan covered with aluminum foil. Use a 12-by-3-inch cake pan to create a water bath for baking the flan in the oven. All pans are available on Amazon and should have a minimum 4-cup capacity. When releasing the flan, if the caramel is hard, it didn't reach the proper temperature; don't consider this a failure, just make more caramel for serving.

VARIATION

Use this recipe and add the extract of your choice: cinnamon, hazelnut, almond, rose, lavender. For coconut flan, use coconut extract and replace the dairy with canned coconut milk (Thai-style works best). For cheese flan, add 1 (8-ounce) bar of cream cheese or Neufchâtel.

PASTEL DE TRES LECHES
THREE MILK CAKE

Origin: Mexico | Vegetarian | Prep time: 30 minutes | Cook time: 30 minutes
Serves 10 to 12

Everyone loves this cake and every household in Mexico has a different way of making it. The commonality is the love poured into crafting the dessert. This recipe is from my mom's recipe box. I still have all her handwritten recipes, and this one is close to my heart. I cannot count how many times my mom baked this cake for birthdays and special celebrations. I recall my first communion fondly, as this cake was served at the celebration luncheon.

For the cake
Butter, for greasing

10 eggs, separated

1 cup refined sugar

1 teaspoon vanilla extract

2 cups all-purpose flour, sifted

For the sauce
1 (14-ounce) can condensed milk

1 (12-ounce) can evaporated milk

1 cup heavy (whipping) cream

1 teaspoon vanilla extract

1 ounce brandy (or 1 teaspoon rum extract for nonalcoholic version)

For the cream
1½ cups heavy (whipping) cream, very cold

½ cup confectioners' sugar, sifted

½ teaspoon powdered vanilla extract or white liquid vanilla extract

1 teaspoon cornstarch or powdered milk

For the decoration
6 to 8 strawberries, halved

1 mango, sliced or cut into small balls

1 to 2 kiwifruit, peeled and sliced

2 mint sprigs

To make the cake

1. Preheat the oven to 375°F. Butter a 13-by-9-inch glass baking dish.

2. In a large bowl or the bowl of a stand mixer, whip the egg whites for 8 minutes until fluffy. Add the sugar, a little bit at a time, and continue whipping until stiff peaks form. Set aside.

3. In a separate large bowl, whip the egg yolks until light yellow. Add the vanilla and whip for another 3 minutes. Gently fold in the whipped whites with a spatula.

4. Add the flour, a little bit at a time, folding it in with slow circular movements to preserve the airiness of the batter. Pour the batter into the prepared pan and smooth the top with the spatula.

5. Bake for 20 to 30 minutes, until golden brown. Avoid opening the oven while the cake is baking, as it could deflate. Insert a wood toothpick, and if it comes out clean, the cake is ready. Set aside to cool completely.

To make the sauce

6. In a medium bowl, combine the condensed milk, evaporated milk, cream, vanilla, and brandy and whisk until combined. Refrigerate the sauce until ready to use.

7. When the cake is cool, use a fork to poke holes all over the top. Pour the sauce evenly over the cake. Refrigerate the cake, covered, for at least 1 hour 30 minutes and up to overnight. The longer, the better.

To make the cream

8. Put the cream in the freezer for 15 minutes. Doing this will allow the cream to whip quickly.

9. Pour the very cold cream into the bowl of a standing mixer and whip on high until it doubles. Add the confectioners' sugar slowly, then incorporate the vanilla and cornstarch. Continue beating for another 2 minutes. Do not overwhip, as the cream can turn into butter. Keep the whipped cream refrigerated until ready to use.

10. Fill a piping bag with the whipped cream and keep it cold using a bowl with ice while doing the piping work. Or use a spatula to cover the cake with the cream.

To make the decoration

11. Decorate the cake with the strawberries, mango, kiwifruit, and mint. Keep the cake refrigerated until ready to serve.

CHURROS DE CANELA
CINNAMON CHURROS

Origin: Mexico | Vegetarian | Prep time: 30 minutes | Cook time: 45 minutes
Serves 10 to 12 | Special equipment: piping bag with star tip

Churros originated in Catalunya, Spain, and were brought to Mexico during the colonization. Some say churros began in China as a breakfast item and were brought to Spain by the Portuguese. Churros are made with a simple wheat dough, fried and sprinkled with cinnamon and sugar. They're pretty popular during the winter served with hot chocolate as an evening snack.

½ cup whole milk

½ cup water

1 tablespoon sugar, plus 1 cup

¼ teaspoon salt

2 tablespoons butter

1 cup flour, sifted

2 eggs, beaten

3 cups canola or corn oil (not peanut)

1 teaspoon ground cinnamon

1. In a soup pot over medium heat, combine the milk, water, 1 tablespoon of sugar, and salt and whisk for 5 to 7 minutes. Add the butter and continue whisking until melted.

2. Turn off the heat and add the flour, a little bit at a time, whisking vigorously until integrated. Add the eggs and whisk again for about 15 minutes, until the dough turns soft and silky. Transfer the dough to a piping bag with a star tip. Set aside.

3. In a large skillet, heat the oil to between 350°F and 360°F. (If not using a thermometer, drop some dough in the oil; if it starts bubbling and browning rapidly, the oil is ready.)

4. You can make straight lines of dough, rounds, or twists. All are acceptable for churros. Fry the churros for 3 to 5 minutes, until golden brown. Use tongs to transfer them to a paper towel–covered plate to remove excess oil.

5. On another plate, mix together the cinnamon and remaining 1 cup of sugar. While the churros are still warm, dredge them in the cinnamon-sugar mixture and serve.

ATOLE DE CALABAZA
PUMPKIN ATOLE

Origin: Hidalgo and Chiapas | Vegetarian | Prep time: 10 minutes
Cook time: 30 minutes | Serves 8

Atole, or atolli, is a traditional dish from pre-Hispanic times. It was made with maize, water, and fruit and served either hot or cold. With the Spaniards' arrival, dairy was added to the diet, and milk replaced the water in the dish. There are different types of atole. The chocolate version is called champurrado and is made with piloncillo, Mexican chocolate, and masa. A savory version called chileatole is made with corn, epazote, and poblano peppers. Pumpkin atole is served during the fall, and the type of pumpkin used is calabaza de Castilla.

8 cups whole milk

1 (8-ounce) piloncillo cone

1 cinnamon stick

1 teaspoon nutmeg (optional)

1 (8-ounce) can pumpkin puree

2 tablespoons cornstarch, diluted in ½ cup water

3 tablespoons roasted pepitas

1. In a saucepan over medium heat, combine the milk, piloncillo, cinnamon, and nutmeg (if using). Cook, continually stirring, for about 15 minutes, or until the piloncillo has dissolved.

2. Whisk in the pumpkin puree. Cook for another 5 to 7 minutes, then add the cornstarch slurry.

3. Keep stirring for another 7 minutes, or until the atole becomes thick. Serve hot, garnished with the pepitas.

VARIATION
Swap the pumpkin for sweet potato, apple puree, strawberry, or guava preserves. If using guava, omit the nutmeg, as it doesn't pair well.

CAPIROTADA
MEXICAN BREAD PUDDING

Origin: Sonora, Sinaloa, Michoacán, Jalisco, Durango, Guanajuato, San Luis Potosí, Zacatecas, Tamaulipas, and Nuevo León | Vegetarian
Prep time: 30 minutes | Cook time: 1 hour 25 minutes | Serves 10 to 12

Capirotada is a dessert typically served during Lent as a way to use leftover bread. There are many versions, but this one is based on my great-grandmother's recipe. She was from Sonora. I have fond memories of her preparing this bread pudding. She used a big clay pot, in which she fried the bread and layered it like a lasagna. She would use candied "biznaga," prunes, plantains, and Chihuahua-style cheese, as that state was my family's home base.

3 tablespoons butter, plus more for greasing

2 bolillos, sliced (or baguette cut into 8 slices)

2 (8- to 9-ounce) piloncillo cones (or 2 cups dark sugar mixed with 4 tablespoons molasses)

4 cups water

1 cinnamon stick

1 star anise

2 cloves

¼ cup raisins (optional)

¼ cup roasted peanuts or almonds

¼ cup pine nuts or pecans

¼ cup coconut shavings

2 cups grated cotija cheese

Milk, for serving

1. Preheat the oven to 375°F. Grease a square glass baking pan with butter and set aside.

2. Butter the bread slices on both sides and lay them on a baking sheet. Bake for 10 minutes, or until toasted. Flip and toast on the other side.

3. In a saucepan over low heat, combine the piloncillo cones, water, cinnamon, star anise, and cloves and cook for 20 minutes, until an amber-colored sugar syrup forms. Add the raisins (if using) and allow them to plump in the syrup for 10 to 15 minutes.

4. Layer the toasted bread in the prepared baking pan. Sprinkle with the peanuts, pine nuts, coconut, and cheese. You can make several layers.

5. Ladle the warm piloncillo syrup and raisins over the top, making sure to drench each piece of the toasted bread on every layer.

6. Cover the pan with aluminum foil and bake for 30 minutes. Remove the foil and toast the top for 10 minutes more. Serve immediately with a glass of milk.

VARIATION

Use toasted croissants cut into chunks. Use an orange peel instead of star anise. Sprinkle the bread pudding with nonpareils to add color. Some home cooks add a few corn tortillas to the bottom of the pan to prevent the bread from burning while baking. Capirotada can be served cold, too, so keep any leftovers in the refrigerator.

MEXICO'S CHRISTMAS FOOD AND TRADITIONS

Las Posadas are street parties leading up to Christmas Day that include processions simulating Maria and Joseph's journey and symbols such as star piñatas representing the seven deadly sins that, when destroyed, provide gifts of sugarcane, mandarins, peanuts, jícama, and colación. Nativity scenes are the pride and joy of many families. Traditional dishes are pozole and ponche de frutas. I grew up eating a turkey dinner, as my family is from the North. However, my Spanish grandfather also included bacalao and turrones on the family menu. In Mexico City, families eat romeritos with shrimp cakes, prune pork loin or pierna adobada, and Christmas salad with beets.

The night before Epiphany, children leave their shoes out overnight to find them full of gifts the next day, and families cut the Rosca de Reyes, which includes at least one baby figurine. The lucky one that finds the baby has to invite everyone for dinner on February 2, the day of La Candelaria, which is when Baby Jesus is officially presented to the community. Tamales, hot chocolate, and atole are traditionally served.

ARROZ CON LECHE

MEXICAN RICE PUDDING

Origin: Mexico City, Guanajuato, Jalisco, Tabasco, and Chiapas | Vegetarian
Prep time: 5 minutes | Cook time: 45 minutes | Serves 6
Special equipment: cast-iron Dutch oven

Rice pudding originated in Asia and from there was adopted by Europe. After the 16th century, it came to Latin America. My grandfather was a refugee from Spain, and my grandmother used to make Asturias-style rice pudding with anisette, as that was the style he enjoyed most. Each household in Mexico has its own family recipe. My mom loved adding orange peel, so I do the same.

1 cup rice (long- or short-grain)

1 cup water

Peel of 1 orange

1 cinnamon stick

Pinch coarse salt

1 tablespoon ground cinnamon, plus pinch for serving

1 (12-ounce) can evaporated milk

1 cup fresh whole milk

1 tablespoon vanilla extract

1 (14-ounce) can condensed milk

1. In a soup pot or cast-iron Dutch oven over medium heat, combine the rice, water, orange peel, cinnamon stick, salt, and ground cinnamon. Cook for 10 minutes, stirring with a wooden spoon.

2. After the first boil, the rice will become creamy. Add the evaporated milk, whole milk, and vanilla and continue to cook, stirring, for another 20 minutes.

3. When the rice is soft to the touch, add the condensed milk and stir again. Cook for another 10 to 15 minutes, until creamy.

4. Remove and discard the orange peel and cinnamon stick. Turn off the heat and cover the pot with the lid. Serve warm or cold, sprinkled with a little ground cinnamon.

TIP

Short-grain rice makes the rice pudding sticky, so use that type of rice if you prefer that texture. Serve the rice pudding with fresh fruit or pour it in a popsicle mold and put it in the freezer to make iced pops.

CAFÉ DE OLLA CON CANELA
HOT POT COFFEE WITH CINNAMON

Origin: Mexico | Vegan | Prep time: 5 minutes | Cook time: 30 minutes | Serves 4
Special equipment: French press

Some say café de olla became popular during the Mexican Revolution. Many believe this recipe is a century old and a staple of campfires where the "Adelitas" (women at the service of the revolution) used to care for the militia. Hot spiced coffee helped people survive the cold nights. It is called "café de olla" because, traditionally, it is prepared using a clay pot over direct flame. Hot pot coffee is also a tradition at funerals and Day of the Dead celebrations.

4 cups water

1 (8-ounce) piloncillo cone

1 cinnamon stick

1 star anise

1 clove

4 to 6 tablespoons ground Mexican coffee

Sugar, for serving (optional)

1. In a saucepan over medium heat, combine the water and piloncillo and cook for 15 minutes, or until the piloncillo has dissolved. Add the cinnamon, star anise, and clove and cook for another 15 minutes. When the preparation reaches the first boil, remove the spices.

2. Put the ground coffee in a French press and pour the hot piloncillo-spiced water over the top. Steep for 3 minutes, then press.

3. Serve hot, add sugar if needed, and enjoy with pastries.

TIP

The coffee can be made using a pour-over technique or strained. Save any leftover coffee to enjoy iced with an orange peel twist.

AGUA DE HORCHATA
HORCHATA

Origin: Mexico | Vegetarian | Prep time: 5 minutes, plus overnight to soak rice
Serves 4 | Special equipment: blender

Horchata is a milky drink that originated in Spain and is commonly served in summer and prepared with nuts called "chufas." In Mexico, this drink is prepared with rice and cinnamon, and it sometimes includes almonds. Street parties and parrilladas always have a perol of agua de horchata. The rice requires soaking overnight.

1 cup rice

¼ cup raw almonds

1 cinnamon stick

1 cup hot water

4 cups water, divided

1 (14-ounce) can condensed milk

1 (12-ounce) can evaporated milk

1 teaspoon vanilla extract

Sugar (optional)

1. In a medium bowl, combine the rice, almonds, cinnamon, and the hot water. Cover with plastic and soak overnight.

2. The next day, transfer the mixture to a blender and add 1 cup of water. Blend the mixture into a watery paste, adding more water if necessary.

3. Strain the rice paste and transfer it to a pitcher. Combine it with the remaining 3 cups of water, the condensed and evaporated milks, and the vanilla. Mix until milky.

4. Taste and add sugar (if using). Serve in a tall glass over ice.

VARIATION

Add a handful of fresh strawberries to make strawberry horchata. This same recipe is perfect for making ice pops or granita. Replace the condensed milk with 1 cup of sugar and use coconut or almond milk for a nondairy option.

AGUA DE JAMAICA
HIBISCUS ICED TEA

Origin: Mexico | Vegan | Prep time: 5 minutes, plus 30 minutes to steep | Serves 6

This hibiscus iced tea is a beverage from my childhood. My mom always had a big pitcher of jamaica agua fresca ready for me to drink after school. This drink is so refreshing and tastes a bit like cranberry juice. Drinking it brings happy thoughts from home. The flower is edible and can be used for other purposes, such as in syrups and as a meat replacement in vegan dishes.

1 cup dried hibiscus flowers

4 cups boiling water

1 liter iced water

2 cups ice

½ cup agave nectar (or raw sugar, granulated sugar, or Splenda)

1. In a mason jar, steep the hibiscus flowers in the boiling water for 30 minutes. Allow the hibiscus flowers to steep long enough to produce a strong tea extract. It can be covered and left in the refrigerator overnight.

2. When ready to serve, pour the iced water into a pitcher and add the ice. Mix with the hibiscus tea extract and sweeten with the agave nectar. Serve cold in a tall glass.

TIP

Make a hibiscus latte by adding your favorite creamer. I recommend sweet coconut milk creamer. Or prepare a hibiscus margarita using the hibiscus tea extract and adding lemonade and tequila.

PONCHE DE FRUTAS PARA LA NAVIDAD
CHRISTMAS FRUIT PUNCH

Origin: Mexico | Vegan | Prep time: 15 minutes | Cook time: 30 minutes | Serves 12

This punch is an excellent drink for parties and a staple for Las Posadas. The beverage is part of the Spanish heritage and uses seasonal fruits such as tejocote and sugarcane. Home cooks prepare a big pot, and everyone can enjoy it after breaking the classic piñata. This hot beverage is a family-friendly option, but some adults like to add *piquete* to their ponche, mixing it with brandy, rum, or tequila.

2 green apples, cored and diced

3 McIntosh apples, cored and diced

2 pears, cored and diced

2 quince, cored and diced

2 Valencia oranges, sliced

8 prunes, pitted

6 dried hibiscus flowers

5 tamarind pods

4 cinnamon sticks

2 cups turbinado sugar

10 cups water

Combine the green and McIntosh apples, pears, quince, oranges, prunes, hibiscus flowers, tamarind, cinnamon, turbinado sugar, and water in a large pot over medium heat. Cook for 30 minutes. Serve the ponche hot and scoop the cooked fruit into the cups.

TIP

For an adult version, add 1 ounce of brandy or rum per cup and use jarritos for serving. Fruit punch leftovers keep well, refrigerated, for up to 3 days. Reheat the ponche in the microwave. On Amazon, there is a Ponche de Navidad kit available that includes all the ingredients needed for the recipe.

MEASUREMENT CONVERSIONS

VOLUME EQUIVALENTS (LIQUID)

US STANDARD	US STANDARD (OUNCES)	METRIC (APPROXIMATE)
2 tablespoons	1 fl. oz.	30 mL
¼ cup	2 fl. oz.	60 mL
½ cup	4 fl. oz.	120 mL
1 cup	8 fl. oz.	240 mL
1½ cups	12 fl. oz.	355 mL
2 cups or 1 pint	16 fl. oz.	475 mL
4 cups or 1 quart	32 fl. oz.	1 L
1 gallon	128 fl. oz.	4 L

VOLUME EQUIVALENTS (DRY)

US STANDARD	METRIC (APPROXIMATE)
⅛ teaspoon	0.5 mL
¼ teaspoon	1 mL
½ teaspoon	2 mL
¾ teaspoon	4 mL
1 teaspoon	5 mL
1 tablespoon	15 mL
¼ cup	59 mL
⅓ cup	79 mL
½ cup	118 mL
⅔ cup	156 mL
¾ cup	177 mL
1 cup	235 mL
2 cups or 1 pint	475 mL
3 cups	700 mL
4 cups or 1 quart	1 L
½ gallon	2 L
1 gallon	4 L

OVEN TEMPERATURES

FAHRENHEIT (F)	CELSIUS (C) (APPROXIMATE)
250°	120°
300°	150°
325°	165°
350°	180°
375°	190°
400°	200°
425°	220°
450°	230°

WEIGHT EQUIVALENTS

US STANDARD	METRIC (APPROXIMATE)
½ ounce	15 g
1 ounce	30 g
2 ounces	60 g
4 ounces	115 g
8 ounces	225 g
12 ounces	340 g
16 ounces or 1 pound	455 g

INDEX

ACKNOWLEDGMENTS

I want to thank my editorial team for their professionalism and dedication while putting together my first cookbook. I have grown as a writer thanks to your feedback and guidance. Without your help, I would not have been able to become a published author.

I am grateful for my family and my husband's support during the creation process. Without your love, I would not have been able to sustain all those long days and nights of recipe testing, culinary research, and writing.

And to all of you food lovers who have been following my steps since I started my culinary journey: Without your continued support, I wouldn't have been inspired to write this book that I hope you will find helpful.

¡Gracias!

ABOUT THE AUTHOR

Adriana Martin is a home chef and founder of AdrianasBestRecipes.com. She is a Latina food writer specializing in recipe development influenced by Mexico's culinary culture and European cuisine. Her grandmother taught her how to cook, and now her mission is to inspire others to make homemade meals. She recently discovered her passion for baking artisanal bread and classic desserts. Adriana also teaches online cooking classes and is a trained food stylist and photographer. She has published thousands of recipes and has collaborated with top brands and prestigious publications since 2011.

LATISM has recognized Adriana as a Top 100 most influential Latina blogger due to her contributions to the blogosphere, social media influence, and involvement with the community to raise awareness about child hunger in Florida's Orlando area.

Hispanicize and Telemundo awarded Adriana with the 2016 Tecla Award for Best Food Content Creator. The Tecla Awards is a national awards program that honors the achievements of top multicultural content creators.

Printed in the USA
CPSIA information can be obtained
at www.ICGtesting.com
LVHW061612200524
780489LV00003B/14

9 781638 786313